Cooking with Krishna

Gluten-Free Vegan Indian Cuisine for the Conscious Eater

Aruna Dawn Grey

Cooking with Krishna
Gluten-Free Vegan Indian Cuisine for the Conscious Eater

Copyright © 2011 Aruna Dawn Grey. All rights reserved. Except as permitted under U.S. Copyright Act of 1976, no part of this publication may be reproduced, distributed, or transmitted in any form or by any means, or stored in a database or retrieval system, without the prior written permission of the author.

Library of Congress Cataloging-in-Publication Data

ISBN-13: 978-1456548872

ISBN-10: 978-1456548872

Printed in the United States of America

Acknowledgements

For Sherrie Taylor, for teaching me that sharing a meal with others is a divine act.

Table of Contents

To the Reader……………………………………………………………….……7

Introduction…………………………………………………………………….13

Breakfast……………………………………………………………………......23

Appetizers…………………………………………………………….......….31

Breads…………………………………………………………………………...55

Soups and Salads…………………………………………………………..65

Side Dishes………………………………………………………...………….79

Main Courses……………………………………………………………….99

Desserts and Beverages………………………………………..……….119

About the Author………………………………………..........................134

Metric Conversion tables for measurements……………………………...135

To The Reader

This cookbook, "Cooking with Krishna", is the result of my spiritual beliefs and how it created a food evolution in my life. As a holistic health practitioner, we speak of body-mind-spirit balance, but most practitioners and programs shy away from the spiritual aspects. No one wants to be preached to, and certainly no practitioner wants to alienate students or clients. I will not share the life events that lead me to my spiritual awakening, other than to declare that what I eat fuels my mind, body, and soul.

I practice Yoga, both the exercise and philosophy, and they have a principle called Ahimsa, non-violence. In walking the path of better health, I developed a stronger connection with my body and my place in the Universe. While yoga poses strengthen the muscles and organs, for me, cooking strengthens the soul. I personally believe the harm I inflict on the animal ultimately creates harm in my body and mind. I am not here to convert anyone, or create a group of readers with a guilty conscience, but that is where I am at in my mindset today.

As a disciple of the great Yogi saint, Paramhansa Yogananda, I was blessed with the opportunity to receive a spiritual name from Swami Kriyananda, one of the last living direct disciples of the Guru, and the organizer of Ananda Church of Self-Realization.

Food is not only a way to nourish ourselves, but a way to offer life, love, and healing to those around us. Dine in the blissful oneness of all life and forever be blessed.

For those of you outside of the United States, please refer to our Metric conversion Index starting on page 135 to assist you in converting our US measurements to metric.

Namaste,

Aruna

Introduction

Dairy Products: To Eat or Not To Eat

While most of us are familiar with lactose intolerance and milk allergies, there are other reasons why more and more individuals are reducing or eliminating dairy from their diets. In this age of environmental awareness, using plant-based milk substitutes is more popular due to their smaller impact on environmental waste. Also, for those who are concerned about animal cruelty, avoiding milk helps reduce factory farming practices. Since most dairy cows are supplied with antibiotics, hormones, and fed food that is laced with pesticides, it may be best if we all took a step away from dairy.

For those of you who are (turning) vegan (choose to eliminate all animal products), dairy allergic, or lactose intolerant, follow the recipes using whatever milk or cheese substitute you wish. You will also find that some recipes call for yogurt, cheese, and/or sour cream. For convenience I will call these "milk product", "vegan sour cream", "non-dairy yogurt" and "vegan cheese" the first time, and from there, just yogurt, milk, etc. If you bought this book because of your gluten/wheat sensitivity and are not following a dairy-free guideline, feel free to use whatever dairy products you wish in equal measure.

I want to take a moment to discuss the flavor of non-dairy products. If you are very new to dairy alternatives, please note that not all dairy-free milks, cheeses, and other products taste the same. While most would say that they could not tell the difference between one brand of 2% milk from another, I assure you there is major variety in texture, flavor, sweetness, etc. between rice and soy milk, and even among the individual brands of soy milk. Be patient, try many brands, and stick with what you love.

In the case of this cookbook, Indian cuisine is often heavy in cream. You can use unsweetened coconut milk, Mimic Crème, or any unflavored, preferably unsweetened, non-dairy milk of choice.

Fats: The Good, The Bad, And The Ugly

Remember when margarine first came out and we thought it was healthful to smear gobs of it on our food to get the healthful polyunsaturated fats? Well, like most other food trends, the good and the bad fats list keeps getting updated. Here is my take on fats, as far as this cookbook is concerned: use what is readily available to you. Traditional Indian fare uses ghee, or clarified butter, which can be made at home or purchased in many stores. However, ghee is not dairy-free and therefore does not belong on a vegan menu. In place of ghee you can use coconut oil, which is solid at room temperature, or any vegan butter, such as Earth Balance, or any cooking oil of choice. If you are allergic to nuts, you may not be able to have coconut, so vegan butter substitutes or oils such as Canola may be best.

Want To Reduce Fat?

While our recipes will be naturally cholesterol-free because we have omitted all animal products, almost all of our recipes contain oil, margarine, cheese, or all. However, most are considered low-fat compared to their original. For those of you who need or want to reduce the fat even more, there are a number of substitutions you can use.

One of the most popular ways to reduce fat is to use less oil or cream and more water. I would prefer to eat a smaller portion of something higher in fat, and then fill up on a low fat salad or soup than not have it at all. Moderation is still the best diet, but know yourself. If you struggle with small portions of rich food, if you need to feel full to feel satisfied, then lower the fat in your cooking. I myself cannot tolerate too much dietary fat, but no two bodies are identical.

Limiting Sodium

While the body does need some sodium, we are being overloaded terribly in this country with the amount that makes its way into our food supply. There are a number of potassium salt products out there for those who must watch their sodium intake. Spices and salt-free spice blends really wake up vegetables and beans, and I honestly like the potassium salts.

However, Indian Black Salt is lower in sodium than traditional salt, so you may want to try this instead. It has a different flavor than traditional salt, so taste it before you substitute it in your meals.

What is Gluten?

As mentioned earlier, gluten is the protein that naturally occurs in the following grains: wheat, rye, barley, durum, semolina, einkorn, graham, bulgur, couscous, spelt, farro, kamut, and triticale. Commercial oats also contain gluten due to cross contamination in processing, but actually are Gluten-Free otherwise. Depending on your level of sensitivity will depend if you can use regular oats or if you need to invest in oats that specifically indicate they are Gluten-Free. I myself am not sensitive enough for the cross-contamination of oats, so I buy regular oats, which are more affordable and certainly easier to obtain. I would consult with your healthcare provider or nutritionist as to whether or not you can handle oats, or any product for that matter, that is processed on equipment or manufactured in the same environment, as a gluten product.

Therefore, gluten will be present in these grains flours and byproducts, such as barley malt, beer, and many flavorings and spices. Gluten is in soy sauce, MSG, and many condiments. It is also in just about every prepackaged vegan "cold cut" and protein product available that I have found. Please read your labels if gluten is off limits. However, living Gluten-Free is not a death sentence. I have baked cookies, breads, cakes, and just about everything else with a Gluten-Free flour or blend of flours. They cost more, but you will need to take less days off of work because of tummyaches, bowel issues, and other nasties. You can buy Gluten-Free bread, pizza dough, and everything imaginable these days.

What Grains and Flours are Gluten-Free?

Corn flour, cornmeal, and cornstarch
Buckwheat and buckwheat flour
Rice flour- white and brown
Quinoa, quinoa cereal flakes, and quinoa flour
Millet and millet flour
Sorghum flour
Amaranth and amaranth flour
Certified Gluten-Free oats and oatmeal
Coconut flour
Teff flour
Nut meals and flours- almond, chestnut, pecan, cashew
Chickpea/Garbanzo (called Besan or Gram in Indian)
Fava bean, Pea, Soy and all other bean flours
Tapioca pearls and tapioca starch/flour (they are the same product)
Potato starch
Potato flour (which is different than potato starch)
Sweet potato and yam flour
Arrowroot starch

Why Eat Wheat/Gluten-Free?

There is a growing awareness that a number of individuals experience mild to severe gastro-intestinal distress when eating wheat/gluten containing foods. While most individuals are more likely to have sensitivity to these foods if eaten in excess, there are those who have allergies to wheat or gluten and therefore cannot safely eat even a small portion of the culprit food.

Another concern is Celiac Disease, a condition in which a person is intolerant to gluten containing foods. In the body of someone with this condition, consuming gluten containing food sets off an autoimmune response that causes damage to the small intestine. This, in turn, causes the small intestine to lose the ability to absorb nutrients, leading to malnutrition, permanent intestinal damage, and possibility of requiring surgery.

There is a belief that removing gluten as well as casein, a protein found in dairy, helps children with Autism Spectrum Disorder. Some parents report improvements in autism symptoms with this dietary regimen. Little actual research has been done, however, on the Gluten-Free/casein-free diet for autism. However, since there is no dietary need for gluten or casein in the diet, so there is no harm in removing them if they help you or your child's health.

For those who find that eating wheat and/or gluten containing foods creates mild to moderate distress, it is recommended to follow an elimination diet and consult with a healthcare provider and/or dietician for further assistance.

Now, on to the best part- eating! For any recipe that offers a gluten-based protein, feel free to substitute lentils, sliced/diced Portabellas, or any other product you desire.

In this book, every single recipe is already Gluten-Free, so you need not be concerned about making any modifications. However, if you buy any already prepared sauces, please read the label. Gluten is present in MSG, soy sauce, and often called natural spices, flavorings, and discreet names. When in doubt, make everything yourself or only buy a product clearly labeled Gluten-Free.

Sugar/Sweeteners

It is not widely known that regular white sugar is almost always processed with animal bones to give it its white color and smooth texture, so unless labeled otherwise, white sugar is not vegan. Therefore, I specify "vegan sugar" if this is important to you.

You should also be warned that honey is not considered vegan, as it is an animal created product. However, the case for honey and its curative benefits is no one I dismiss, as consuming small amounts of local honey can help diminish severe allergic reactions to bee stings and other seasonal allergies. Since I am one of those people who needs to go to the Emergency Room if she gets a bee sting, and given my rural living arrangements, I have made a conscious choice to purchase and use limited amounts (less than a Tablespoon) of honey from a small, local supplier in my country town. Since this practice, my last bee sting did not lead to a health crisis, and some natural topical anti-itch preparation was all that I needed, rather than shots and oxygen. I will leave it up to you to choose to use honey or not.

As for other sweeteners, you can choose agave nectar (from a cactus), true maple syrup, more natural sugars such as date, evaporated cane crystals, or turbinado. Do keep in mind that all of these mentioned do have a sugar count and may not be suitable for Diabetics. This often leads the cook to decide whether to omit their use entirely or rely on more processed, artificial sweeteners.

As for as sweeteners that do not affect Diabetics, Stevia, from a plant, has zero calories, and is not truly therefore seen as artificial. You may also consider Xylitol, Splenda, Nutrasweet, and Saccharin. All of these have their ups and downs, and I listed them in order of what appears to be product safety. Read labels and make your choices based on your body. You will need to decide if using artificial sweeteners fits your overall dietary plan, or if using very small amounts of a more natural sweetener with a natural sugar count in moderation is best.

Indian Cooking Basics

Indian cuisine is quite different from American and European cooking. Just like Indian culture, the food of India has been influenced by various civilizations which have contributed their overall development.

Foods of India are distinctly known for their spiciness. Throughout India, be it North India or South India, spices are used generously in food. All spices contain vitamins and nutrients, and are healing in nature. Some spices maintain health, while others are restorative in nature. The Indians are forerunners of the use of herbs and spices for maintaining and correcting imbalances.

For those of you outside of the United States, please refer to our Metric conversion Index starting on page135 to assist you in converting our US measurements to metric.

Helpful Tips for Successful Indian Cooking

Read the recipe before starting and make sure all ingredients are ready. I did my best to select recipes that use a lot of the same ingredients, so you are not constantly running to the market or mail ordering something new. You initially may need to purchase or order some spices to create authentic Indian recipes, but a little goes a long way, and vegan fare is lower in cost than stocking meat and dairy, so you will be ahead in the long run.

When frying, make sure you use an oil meant for high heat (coconut, safflower, peanut, etc.) and make sure the oil is heated to the correct temperature. Oil that is too cool will create soggy food than is much higher in fat content than oil that is hotter. Drain all fried foods on towels before serving whenever possible. I will remind you of this in every recipe that calls for deep frying, so not to worry.

Make sure to select the right size pan. If a pan is very small proportionally to the food you are preparing, it will be difficult to evenly cook the food. Using a pan that is too big will cause the liquid in the food to evaporate too quickly.

Measuring vegetables and fruits using cup measurements can vary depending on whether raw, chopped, or cooked foods are used. For everyday purposes, it is best to approximate measurements. Remember the cup measurements are just guidelines.

Indian is among the leading cuisines of the world and is not as difficult to prepare as you may think. Contrary to popular belief, Indian food is not just about Curry and unsweetened coconut milk, but they can dominate in a vegan diet. At the same time, Indian cuisine is not just for vegetarians/vegans, so when finding a new recipe, read to make sure you are prepared to make necessary substitutes for ghee, cream, and meat.

'Curry' is synonymous with Indian food is thought of as its key ingredient. This all-important powder is actually a mix of spices collectively known as Garam Masala and is added to dishes along with other spices to enhance their flavor and aroma. Beginners may simply purchase Garam Masala and Curry and call it a day, or purchase some of the individual spices that are mentioned a little later on in this chapter.

Indian spices can be bought in most supermarkets. What can't be found there is always available in Indian or Asian grocery stores. The internet will also be your most gracious host in locating whatever else you may need.

Most Indian food does not require special cooking utensils so there is no need for those starting out to buy too many things. A basic set of pots, knives, bakeware, and if you want to splurge, a bamboo steamer, is all you will need to make any of the recipes featured in this cookbook

Indian Herbs and Spices

There are a many Indian spices available. Those marked with * indicate ones I recommend stocking for your beginner's Indian pantry.

Ajwain

Ajwain, also known as carom seeds, look and smell much like cumin seeds, Ajwain seeds are pungent. Ajwain compliments dhals, breads, and root vegetables. In herbal healing, they comfort diarrhea and stomach pains and are an excellent aid to digestion.

Asafetida (hing)

Asafetida (Hing) is very common ingredient in Indian cooking, often found in Biryani and other rice dishes. Hing has very strong and unique smell and flavor. It is a staple in Ayurvedic medicine and good for digestive system. I personally do not care for hing, so I have limited its use.

Black Cardamom (kali elaichi)

Black cardamom is a southern India spice and is an important ingredient of the Indian spice mixture Garam Masala.

Black Pepper (kali mirch)*

Originally from India, Black pepper is used around the world as a main flavoring agent. It creates heat in the body and is a lovely stimulant for circulation.

Black salt (kala namak)

Black salt is used extensively in Indian cuisine as well as in Ayurvedic medicine. It tastes different than regular "table salt" and is often used by people with high blood pressure or sodium restricted diets because it does not contain significant amounts of sodium. It is also used to relieve both heartburn and flatulence.

Cilantro*

Cilantro is an herb commonly found in Mexican and Indian dishes, and is sometimes referred to as Mexican parsley. It is related to coriander, which is the ground seed of the leafy cilantro plant.

Cinnamon (dalchini)*

The sweet aroma and warm taste of cinnamon make very unique spice for cooking or baking. Cinnamon has unique anti-clotting action and is used to control blood sugar as reliably as many diabetic medications. A flavorful component in chai tea, cinnamon also boosts the immune system and is antibiotic in nature.

Cloves (long)*

India's traditional ayurvedic healers have used cloves since ancient times to treat respiratory and digestive ailments. Cloves are said to have a positive effect on stomach ulcers, vomiting, flatulence, and to stimulate the digestive system.

Coriander (dhania)

Coriander is an ingredient of Garam Masala and pickling spices. Coriander seed oil is an aromatic stimulant, a carminative (remedial in flatulence), an appetizer and a digestive stimulating the stomach and intestines. It is generally beneficial to the nervous system.

Cumin seed (jeera)*

This is a very essential herb for cooking and I recommend you stock this herb. It is very aromatic, used in Ayurvedic medicine in India. It is said that cumin seed helps in headaches, nausea and liver problems.

Fennel seed (saunf)

The bulb, foliage, and seeds of the fennel plant are widely used in many of the culinary traditions of the world. Dried fennel seed is an aromatic, it is commonly used to treat asthma, bronchitis, colic disease, food poisoning and motion sickness

Fenugreek (methi)

Fenugreek seed, commonly called methi, is frequently used in the preparation of pickles and Curry powders. Fenugreek is mainly used as digestive aid. It is ideal for treating sinus, lung congestion, reduces inflammation and fights infection, but is equally used along with cinnamon to control blood sugar.

Ginger (adrak)*

Ginger is essential to Indian cooking, but working. A very potent spice, always use less than you think you need, and chop it as finely as possible. While it is not as potent medicinally, feel free to use powdered ginger at any time.

Green Cardamom (elaichi)

Green Cardamom is mostly used in sweets to give nice aroma and flavor, and is a main component to chai tea and desserts.

Mustard seed (rai)

Dry mustard seed has no aroma but its rather potent, hot flavor is released when it mixes with water. It is often used in Indian cooking specially for chaunk and pickling.

Red Chili powder/Cayenne (lal mirch)*

Red chilies are used in Indian cooking as one of the main spice. Red chilies are used whole, crushed or in powder form. The seeds yield the hottest spiciness, and you may wish to wear gloves when working with the fresh seeds. You may use cayenne pepper in powder or flakes instead of working with the fresh peppers.

Saffron (kesar)

Saffron is used in cooking as a seasoning and coloring agent. Saffron oil has therapeutic properties. In India, saffron is used in winter because it provides heat. It is the most expensive spice on the market today, and a few strands can cost in excess of $40 depending on the season. It is a luxury spice, so reserve it for your most special meals.

Tamarind (imli)

Tamarind's acidic, juicy pulp is used to flavor a variety of foods. It is used as a souring agent in indian lentil dishes, curries and chutneys, where its flavor is more authentic than vinegar or lemon juice.

Turmeric (haldi)*

Turmeric is an ancient spice, a native of southeast Asia, commonly used in curries, dyes, and as a condiment. It is still used in rituals of the Hindu religion. Turmeric is a mild digestive. Turmeric is perhaps the most common spice used in Indian cooking and is a must stock for your pantry.

Pantry Staples and Helpful Tools

In addition to the spices recommended on the previous pages, there are a few other items that are highly recommended to stock in your Indian pantry:

Dry goods: Besan (sometimes called Gram) which is the same as chickpea or garbanzo flour, All-Purpose Gluten-Free flour, basmati rice, coconut oil, canned unsweetened coconut milk, oil for high heat cooking, canned tomatoes, dried lentils in brown and red, kidney beans, chickpeas whether canned or dried, vegan-appropriate sweetener/sugar(most sugar is ground with animal bones, and is not considered truly vegan),non-stick cooking spray and Mimic Crème (these last two are very helpful, but not required).

Perishable goods: Tofu, tempeh, vegan butter, non-dairy milk of choice, and of course, seasonal produce.

Required Kitchen Tools: a good knife, cutting board, an assortment of pots/pans, baking sheets, and a strainer/colander. A bamboo steamer is helpful, but not required, as is a crock pot/slow cooker.

How to Make Vegan Paneer

Paneer is a delicious homemade Indian cheese and is used in many different recipes from desserts to appetizers to main course dishes alike. The problem with Paneer is that it is dairy, and regardless of your reasons, is unsuited for a vegan cookbook. I went to every store in an hour radius of my home in search of vegan Paneer, even contacting two very authentic and sympathetic Indian restaurants. I realized I was not going to be able to find one already made for me in the Midwest and I would either need to omit it or make it myself.

To my relief, like many vegan staples (almond milk for instance), it is quite easy to make.

As I am unaware of any commercially available vegan Paneer in other regions, I wanted to provide this simple recipe and suggest you try it. If you have ever tasted real Paneer, you may be quite surprised at how much it is in likeness and texture to the real thing. If you do not care for it, feel free to omit from recipes or substitute vegan Mozzarella or other cheese product of choice.

Paneer Recipe

For those of you outside of the United States, please refer to our Metric conversion Index starting on page135 to assist you in converting our US measurements to metric.

8 cups any unsweetened, plain milk product of choice

¼ cup freshly squeezed lemon juice

½ cup hot water

Mix lemon juice in half cup of hot water and put aside.

Boil the milk over medium heat, stirring occasionally, making sure not to burn. As it comes to a boil, add the lemon juice and water mixture gradually, stirring gently. If done correctly, this will create a curdlike substance, similar to cottage cheese in appearance.

Wrap the curds in a piece of muslin or cheesecloth and rinse under cold water, squeezing well. You should press the Paneer under a heavy weight for about one hour for dessert Paneer, and two hours for any other type of Paneer, much like how you would press tofu to remove excess liquid. It should emerge in a cakelike shape. Paneer can be refrigerated for you to 2 days or kept frozen for 3 months.

If Paneer will be used to make desserts or sweets, following these instructions:

To check if the right amount of water is out of the Paneer, take a little piece of Paneer on your palm and rub with your fingers. After rubbing the Paneer for about 15-20 seconds, you should be able to make a firm but smooth ball.

If Paneer will be used for making any other meals:

Before pressing, knead Paneer to prevent it from crumbling. Cut the Paneer into desired shape and size.

For variety, you can season or spice your Paneer while pressing. Dessert Paneer may be pressed with cinnamon, sweetener, and cardamom whereas appetizer Paneer may be flavored with Curry, cloves, salt and pepper, etc.

How to Make Vegan Yogurt

While vegan yogurt is readily available, it may be hard to find one made without soy. I have also found that more than one soy yogurt uses real dairy bacteria/cultures, so for me, that is just not dairy-free enough for my use.

Homemade yogurt made from almond or rice milk tastes delicious and is very refreshing. It is also relatively easy to make, easy to flavor, and very inexpensive. Yogurt made from leftover yogurt tastes better and has more cultures from batch to batch than the first batch.

While you can use store bough yogurt as the starter, it has been my experience that they simply do not yield the best results. Even with organic unflavored soy yogurt, I have found the results somewhat disappointing. I suggest your very first batch to be made from dry starter, then use yogurt leftover from this initial batch for future yogurts.

Vegan Yogurt Recipe

For those of you outside of the United States, please refer to our Metric conversion Index starting on page135.

3½ cups milk of choice

2 Tablespoons of any other vegan yogurt, or store bought yogurt starter*

Thermometer to check temperature of milk, optional

Boil the milk and let it cool down to 110°F. You can use a candy thermometer to check the temperature, or remove from heat once it begins to boil If the milk gets too hot it kills the bacteria in the culture, so you do not want it heat it past the boiling point.

After milk cools down pour into a bowl or container for storage. Add 2 Tablespoons of yogurt. *If using starter, package will tell you how much dry starter to use. Don't follow any other directions from the dry starter package when using this recipe. You may need to scale down the amount of starter for the amount of milk being used, or simply increase the amount of milk.

Mix the yogurt/starter with the milk and stir gently. Cover the bowl with a cloth and keep it in warm place for about 4 hours.

After yogurt is set, refrigerate for at least an hour before using.

Indian Condiments

The two primary condiments you will encounter in Indian Cuisine are Raita and Chutney. Raita is yogurt-based and used as a sauce or dip. Chutney is a very popular relish-like condiment made from fruit, vinegar, sugar and spices. Its texture can range from smooth to chunky and its flavor from mild to hot. I suggest making them in bulk once you find a recipe you like. I prefer to make a lot, and then either jar it and give it away, or store for later use. Chutney and Raita can be used with appetizers, but also for dipping breads or simply spooned on top of any vegetable or main course.

Cucumber Raita

2 large cucumbers, peeled, seeded, and thinly sliced
2 cups plain vegan yogurt
3 Tablespoons lemon juice
2 Tablespoons chopped fresh mint
½ teaspoon vegan sugar or other sweetener of choice
¼ teaspoon coarse salt

Stir together the cucumber, yogurt, lemon juice, mint, sugar, and salt in a bowl. Cover and refrigerate at least 3 hours, preferably overnight.

Tamarind Chutney

1 Tablespoon oil
1 teaspoon cumin seeds
1 teaspoon ground ginger
½ teaspoon cayenne pepper
½ teaspoon fennel seeds
½ teaspoon Garam Masala
2 cups water
1¼ cups vegan sugar
3 tablespoons tamarind paste

Heat the oil in a saucepan over medium heat. Add the cumin seeds, ginger, red chili powder, fennel seeds, and Garam Masala. Cook and stir for about 2 minutes to release the flavors.

Stir the water into the pan with the spices and add the sugar and tamarind paste. Bring to a boil, then simmer over low heat until the mixture turns a deep brown, about 20 to 30 minutes. The sauce will be thin, but it will thicken when cool.

Pineapple and Mango Chutney

Mango Chutney is made from unripe, or green, mangoes, and I really do not care for that. Use ripe mangoes and it provides an entirely different flavor. This is my favorite chutney by far.

2 Tablespoons oil
1 teaspoon crushed red pepper flakes
1 large sweet onion, diced
2 Tablespoons of minced fresh ginger root
1 large yellow pepper, diced
3 large ripe mangoes, peeled, pitted, and diced
1 small pineapple, peeled and diced
½ cup sugar or other sweetener of choice
1 Tablespoon curry powder
½ cup apple cider vinegar

Heat the oil in a large saucepan over medium heat. Stir in the red pepper flakes and cook until they begin to sizzle, then stir in the onions. Reduce heat to low, cover, and cook, stirring occasionally until the onions have softened, about 20 minutes.

Remove the lid, increase the heat to medium, and stir in the ginger and yellow bell pepper. Cook and stir until the ginger is fragrant, 2 to 3 minutes. Stir in the mangoes, pineapple, sweetener, curry powder, and vinegar. Bring to a simmer, and cook for 30 minutes, stirring occasionally. Cool the chutney completely when done and store in airtight containers in the refrigerator.

Breakfasts

Aloo Puha

Westerns will learn right away that Indian breakfasts are very different than what we are used to. While you may not yet be adventurous enough to swap your oatmeal for spicy rice, I really do suggest you try. Spices wake up the metabolism and the nutrients from cooked grains, especially when vegetables are added, sustain you far more than many of our sweet and instant meals.

2 cups cooked rice, any variety
1 Potato, cubed, peeled if desired
1 large yellow Onion, chopped coarsely
2 Green Chilies
¼ cup cooked lentils or prepared dhal
¼ teaspoon Mustard Seeds
½ cup spinach or any other leafy green of choice
1 pinch of Curry powder
2 teaspoons of Peanuts or other nuts (optional)
4 Tablespoons of Oil
1 pinch Turmeric powder
The juice of 1 lemon
Salt and pepper, to taste

Soak the cooked rice in water for at least 30 minutes, or overnight. Wash and drain. Stir in 1 Tablespoon oil, as well as salt, turmeric powder, and Curry, and set aside.

Peel and cut the potato into small cubes. Chop the onions and chilies into desired size pieces.

Heat remaining oil and place lentils mustard seeds, peanuts and greens into a large frying pan over medium heat, stirring frequently, until the seeds begin to pop and sizzle.

Add potatoes, onion, and chilies and cook till they are done, approximately 20 minutes.

Add rice and reduce heat. Stir frequently to prevent sticking. Cook for 5- 7 minutes, or until rice is hot. Remove from heat and add lemon juice just before serving.

Green Rice

This is a hearty breakfast on a really cold day.

Serves 4

1 cup cooked rice, any variety
1 cup of leafy greens of choice
2 cups yogurt
2 Tablespoons oil
¼ cup milk product of choice
1 Green chili, diced
1 teaspoon mustard seeds
1½ teaspoons fresh minced ginger root
2 Tablespoons dried coconut
½ teaspoon salt

In a saucepan, heat oil and mustard seeds over medium heat.

When the mustard seeds start popping add in the ginger, coriander, and green chilies.

Reduce heat and stir in greens. Let sauté for 3-5 minutes, until wilted.

Add rice, salt and coconut. Reduce heat to low and simmer 3-5 minutes until warm.

Just before serving, stir in yogurt and milk. Top with optional nuts.

Punjabi Pakora

Certainly not a traditional breakfast for Americans, but these Pakora are spicy and flavorful and will hold you until lunch.

Serves 2

8 Green Chilies *or* okra
Oil for frying

For the filling
1 Boiled Potato
½ teaspoon Red Chili powder
1 teaspoon finely chopped mint leaves
¼ teaspoon ground ginger
Salt and pepper, to taste

For the topping
1 cup Besan/Gram (Chickpea flour)
3 Tablespoons Rice flour, white or brown
¼ teaspoon Red chili powder
A pinch of Turmeric
A pinch of baking soda
Water to mix topping, as needed

Wash, wipe, and cut the chilies/okra lengthwise and remove seeds.

Mix all the ingredients for the filling and stuff the chilies/okra.

Mix all the ingredients for the topping and add enough water to prepare a thick batter.

Prepare frying pan with 3 inches oil for deep frying, or prepare a deep fryer to 375°F. Oil is ready when a small drop of batter creates splattering.

Dip the stuffed chilies/okra one at a time in batter and fry in hot oil till it is golden in color, usually 1-2 minutes on each side. Flip halfway through cooking. Drain well. Serve hot with chutney.

Rava Uttapam

These spicy fritters are commonly served with dhal (lentils) but you can substitute any other beans and/or vegetables of your choice.

Serves

2 cups chickpea flour
1 cup Paneer, preferably homemade
1 teaspoon salt
¼ teaspoon Red chili powder
3 onions, chopped
2 tomatoes, diced
½ teaspoon of ground ginger
2 green chilies
Oil for cooking
1 teaspoon coriander

Mix chickpea flour with enough water to make a thick batter. Add salt, coriander, ginger, and cayenne to batter. Cover and leave while preparing rest of ingredients.

Finely chop Paneer, onions, tomatoes, and chilies, and mix into batter.

Coat a medium frying pan with 1 inch oil. Pour batter into frying pan, just like pouring pancakes, a few at a time.

Allow to cook about 3-5 minutes, or until the bottom side is browned and the top is set. Flip gently and continue to cook until done.

Pyaz Ki Kachori

Kachori are popular snacks in Indian and Pakistan that are often served at breakfast.

Serves 4

For the dough
1 cup Gluten-Free All-Purpose flour
1 cup besan/chickpea flour
1 teaspoon of Xanthan or Guar gum
¼ cup melted vegan butter or coconut oil
½ teaspoon salt

For filling
2 cups finely chopped onions
1 teaspoon cumin seeds
2 teaspoons fennel seeds
2 Tablespoons Besan/chickpea flour
2 teaspoons coriander
2 teaspoons chili powder
1 teaspoon Garam Masala
2 Tablespoons oil
Salt and pepper to taste

Other Ingredients
Oil for frying

Combine all the dough ingredients in a bowl and add just enough water to create dough. Need until it forms a ball. Divide the dough into 12 equal parts. Set aside.

Heat a small amount oil in a heavy frying pan over medium heat. Add all filling ingredients except the besan. Cook until onions begin to brown, about 5-7 minutes. Remove from heat.

Roll out each portion into a 2 inch circle. Place one portion of the filling in the center. Stretch dough from each side over filling to cover. Seal the ends tightly and remove any excess dough. Flatten slightly by gently press the centre of the Kachori with your thumb.

Heat at least 3 inches of oil in a heavy skillet to 375°F. Deep fry the Kachoris until golden brown, about 3-5 minutes. The Kachoris should puff as they cook.

Veggie Uthappam

A dish where you make all the ingredients into a spiced batter and fried.

Serves 4

2 cups rice
1 cup red lentils
3 medium yellow onions, diced
2 tomatoes, diced
¼ teaspoon ground ginger
2 green chilis, diced
1 teaspoon coriander
1 cup shredded green cabbage
2 carrots, chopped
1½ teaspoons salt
Oil for cooking

Soak rice and lentils separately for 6 hours or overnight.

Drain, then grind the rice and the lentils separately into its own flour. Mix them together after grinding, then add salt.

Cover and let rest for at least 12 hours. This will create a natural fermentation process.

Finely chop onions, green chilis, and tomatoes. Add coriander.

Grate carrots and cabbage, and mix all vegetables into the batter.

Coat a medium frying pan with oil over medium heat. Pour batter into pan like pancakes, and cook until top is set and bottoms begin to brown. Carefully flip and repeat. Serve warm with chutney or raita.

Appetizers

Achari Paneer

Achari Paneer is very versatile and can be served as an appetizer or side dish.

Serves 8

1 pound our recipe Paneer, cut in ½ inch cubes
1 teaspoon salt
¼ teaspoon turmeric
¼ cup plain vegan yogurt
2 Tablespoons oil
¼ teaspoon cumin seeds
1 teaspoon coriander seeds
½ teaspoon black pepper
½ teaspoon fennel seeds
1 ½ cups spinach leaves or other salad greens

Mix Paneer, yogurt, turmeric, and salt. Set aside.

In a frying pan over medium heat, dry roast cumin, coriander seeds, fennel seeds, and black pepper for 1-2 minutes. Crush the roasted seeds using a mortar or rolling pin. Set aside.

Increase to medium heat; add Paneer mixture. Cook for 3-4 minutes or until most of the moisture has evaporated. Do not overcook the Paneer as it will become dry. Remove from heat.

Add all the dry spices and mix well.

Serve warm over a bed of spinach leaves or other greens.

Gingered Asparagus

This is a beautiful dish to serve on holidays and makes a great main course by adding tempeh or tofu.

Serves 4

1 pound of asparagus tips
½ cup sliced mushrooms
2 Tablespoons coconut oil
1 teaspoon cumin seed
1 Tablespoon ginger root, minced, or ½ teaspoon ground ginger
2 teaspoon lemon juice
Salt and pepper to taste

Holding the stalk at both ends, bend gently until it breaks on its own. Discard the hard portion of the stalk.

Cut the remaining asparagus spears diagonally into 2 inch pieces.

Bring oil to medium heat in a large frying pan and sauté mushrooms for 3-5 minutes, or until soft.

Add cumin seeds and heat until they pop.

Add asparagus, ginger, lemon juice, and salt and pepper.

Stir-fry for about 4 to 5 minutes, or until asparagus is desired level of tenderness.

Paares

Often referred to as crackers, Paares make a great crunchy and spicy snack.

Serves 4

1 cup Gluten-Free All-Purpose flour
1 cup chickpea flour
2 Teaspoons Xanthan or Guar gum
4 Tablespoons oil
1 ¼ teaspoons salt
1 teaspoon red chili flakes, optional
¼ teaspoon carom seeds (ajwain)
½ cup water or add as needed to make batter
Oil for frying

Mix flours, gum, salt, pepper, carom seeds, chili flakes, and oil. Add water as needed to make dough. Cover and set aside for at least ten minutes.

Knead the dough and divide into four equal parts. Shape each portion into a flat ball. Roll each into a 6 inch circle. Prick them with a fork several times to prevent puffing while frying.

Cut each of the rolled dough into about half inch wide and 3 inch long pieces. Note: you can cut them in your desire shape.

Heat two inches of oil in a frying pan over medium heat. To check if the oil is ready, drop a small piece of dough in the oil. The dough should make the oil sizzle and float up to the surface .

Make sure to only cook a few at a time so you can turn them over easily and not lower the temperature of the oil when frying. Fry until both sides are golden. Drain and allow to sit for a few minutes.

Paares become crunchy after they cool. Serve with chutney or optional sauces.

Pakoras

Pakoras were one of my favorite appetizers. This was the first Indian recipe I converted to Gluten-Free and no one I have served it to has noticed.

Makes 12

4 slices of Gluten-Free bread, toasted
1 cup gram/besan flour (chickpea flour)
1 Tablespoon rice flour
1 teaspoon salt
Pinch of asafetida
1 teaspoon cumin seeds
2 finely chopped green chilies, seeded
½ cup of water
Oil for frying

Toast bread and remove the crust. Slice the bread lengthwise into 3 equal parts.

Mix all the dry ingredients together. Add the water slowly to make a smooth batter. Add the green chilies and mix well.

Heat the oil in a small frying pan on medium high heat. Frying pan should have at least 2 inches oil. To check if the oil is ready, put one drop of batter in the oil. The batter should come up but not change color right away.

Dip the bread slices in the batter one at a time and slowly drop into the frying pan.

Fry the Pakoras one at a time for about 2 minutes, turn, and repeat on other side.

Chola Tikki

Chola Tikki (chickpeas patties) are another popular spicy appetizer. Tikkis are also known as chaat.

Makes 8

1 cup of chickpeas, cooked, rinsed, and drained
3 medium potatoes, peeled
1 Tablespoon ginger root, minced *or* ½ teaspoon ground ginger
1 Tablespoon chopped cilantro
1 chopped green chili, seeded
½ teaspoon black pepper
1 teaspoon salt
1 teaspoon lemon juice
Oil for frying

Boil potatoes until they are tender, allow to cool, and mash.

Drain the water out of the chickpeas and dry them to remove any excess moisture.

Mash the chickpeas coarsely, allowing for small bits of bean to remain.

Mix potatoes, chickpeas, and all remaining ingredients together.

Divide batter into 8 equal portions, about a half inch thick.

Heat three inches of oil in a medium sized frying pan over medium-high heat.

Place the Tikkis in the pan and fry both sides until both sides are golden brown.

Spicy Chickpeas

Serves 8

2 (15 ounce) cans of chickpeas, rinsed and drained
2 Tablespoons oil
¼ cup gram/besan flour (chickpea flour)
1 teaspoon black *or* regular salt
½ teaspoon black pepper
1 Tablespoon Garam Masala
1 Tablespoon lemon juice

Wash and drain the chickpeas.

Heat the oil in a saucepan over medium heat, add the flour, cooking for 1-2 minutes or until it begins to brown.

Add the chickpeas to the gram flour.

Add salt/black salt, black pepper, and Garam Masala. Stir gently.

Cook on low heat for 10 minutes. Remove from heat. And add lemon juice. Mix gently.

Let the chickpeas sit for at least 30 minutes to absorb all the flavors. The mixture will thicken as it cools.

Spinach Pakoras

Spinach Pakoras can be served many different ways and they always taste great.

Makes 2 dozen

Batter
½ cup chickpea flour
1 Tablespoon corn starch *or* arrowroot *or* potato starch
½ teaspoon salt
½ teaspoon cumin seeds
¼ teaspoon black pepper
About ¾ cup water

Other Ingredients
24 fresh spinach leaves
Oil for frying

Mix all the dry batter ingredients together. Slowly add the water to make a thin batter. You may not need the entire amount.

Heat two inches of oil in a frying pan on medium high heat. To check if the oil is ready, put one drop of batter in oil. The batter should come up but not change color right away.

Dip a spinach leaf into the batter one at a time, making sure it is covered completely in batter. Slowly drop in the slices into the frying pan. Fry in small batches, no more than 4-6 at a time. The Pakoras will take about 2 to 3 minutes to cook. Turn and fry until both sides are golden-brown.

Dahi Vada

Dahi Vadas are lentil dumplings topped with spicy yogurt and chutney.

Makes about 30

For Vadas
1 cup dry brown lentils
Oil for frying

For Garnish
2 cups vegan plain yogurt
1 teaspoon salt
1 teaspoon turmeric powder
3 Tablespoons tamarind or other chutney

Wash dry lentils several times until the water appears clear. Soak in 4 cups of water for at least six hours or overnight.

Drain the water and process lentils in a blender or food processor, adding a small amount of water as needed until mixture is creamy.

To fry, fill a medium frying pan with ½ inch oil. Turn the heat on medium high. To check if oil is ready put a little batter into the oil, oil will sizzle and batter should start expending upwards slowly without changing color.

Place about 1 Tablespoon of batter at a time into the oil. Batter should not be covered with oil. Fry in small batches, 3 or 4 at a time, until golden on both sides.

After you have made all of the Vadas, place on towels to drain for a few minutes.

To make Yogurt topping and Garnish
Stir yogurt until very smooth. Stir in turmeric. Transfer Vadas into a serving dish, spooning some yogurt over each one.

Just before serving, add a bit of tamarind or other chutney.

Muthia

Steamed dumplings, traditionally made with chickpea flour, cabbage and spices. You will need a bamboo or other steamer device for best results.

Serves 4

½ teaspoon agave nectar or other sweetener of choice
4 cups very finely shredded cabbage
1 cup chickpea flour
2 Tablespoons Gluten-Free All-Purpose flour
1 teaspoon cumin seed
½ teaspoon turmeric
1 teaspoon salt
1 teaspoon Xanthan or Guar gum
2 Tablespoons oil

Combine chickpea flour, Gluten-Free flour, gum, cumin seed, turmeric, sweetener, oil, and salt in a bowl.

Add cabbage and stir until it turns into a soft dough.

Divide the mixture into 12 pieces and steam in batches covered, 15 to 20 minutes. Muthias are done when toothpick inserted into the center comes out clean.

Let the Muthias cool off and then slice them in half.

Serve hot with your choice of chutney or yogurt.

Gatte Ke Kadhi

These are steamed dumplings, cooked in spicy gravy.

Serves 4

For the Gattes (dumplings)
1 ¼ cup chickpea flour
½ teaspoon red chili powder
½ teaspoon salt
¼ teaspoon turmeric
3 Tablespoons vegan yogurt
3 Tablespoons oil

For the Kadhi (gravy)
1 cup vegan yogurt
1 Tablespoon chickpea flour
¼ teaspoon turmeric
1 Tablespoon coriander
1 teaspoon salt
2 Tablespoons oil
1 teaspoon cumin seeds

Mix all the dumpling ingredients in a bowl to make dough. If needed, add a small amount of water.

Divide dough into 4 parts and roll each into a log. Each log should be approximately 5 inches in length and about 1 inch in diameter. You can oil your palms to keep dough from sticking to your hands.

Bring 3 cups of water to a boil in a large pot. Gently drop logs into the water and cook until they float up to the surface, about 5 minutes. Remove from water to cool and drain, about 10 minutes. Slice the logs into 1 inch pieces. Set aside.

Mix yogurt and chickpea flour into a paste. Add turmeric and coriander.

Add oil to a saucepan over medium heat. Add the cumin, salt, and mustard seeds and roast until they begin to pop. Pour in the yogurt paste and stir for approx. 2 minutes. Add 3 cups of water and stir until the gravy comes to a boil. Add the Gatte to the gravy, cover and let simmer on low-medium heat for 20 minutes before serving.

Potato Paneer

Makes 48

4 large russet potatoes
2 cups mashed Paneer *or* any other vegan cheese, shredded
2 teaspoons salt
½ teaspoon black pepper
1/3 cup potato flour (**not** starch) or any other Gluten-Free flour
2/3 cup water
½ teaspoon Curry powder
Oil for frying

Mix flour and water together to make a thin batter. Set aside.

Peel potatoes and shred with a cheese grater or food processor. Bring 4 cups of water to a boil, add potatoes and reduce heat, simmering until tender, normally just 2-4 minutes. Drain and allow to cool.

Carefully squeeze out any excess water out of the potatoes, again making sure to not make the shredded potatoes mushy.

Combine potatoes, mashed Paneer or cheese, Curry, and salt. Stir gently to incorporate all ingredients without mashing up the potatoes. Divide the potato mixture in about 48 small patties. Set aside.

Heat two inches of oil in a frying pan over medium-high heat. To check if the oil is ready, put one small piece of mix into the oil, it should sizzle and come up right away.

Drop one patty at a time into the batter, coating both sides, and slowly drop into the frying pan. To maintain the oil's temperature, do not fry too many at one time. Fry until golden on both sides. Drain on paper towels.

Serve with ketchup, chutney, or desired condiment of choice.

Khasta Kachori

Khasta Kachori are spicy, fried puffed pastries commonly served as an appetizer.

Makes 12

Ingredients for crust
1 cup chickpea flour
¼ teaspoon salt
2 Tablespoons oil
¼ cup cold water

Ingredients for filling
¼ cup yellow split peas or any variety of lentils
1 teaspoon coarsely grinded fennel seeds
1 teaspoon coarsely grinded coriander seeds
¼ teaspoon ground ginger
½ teaspoon salt
1 Tablespoon oil
2 Tablespoons water
Oil for frying

To make crust
Mix the flour, salt and oil.

Add the chilled water slowly, stirring as you add. Do not knead or overly stir the dough. The dough should be soft. Cover and let it sit for at least 30 minutes.

To make filling
Grind the peas or lentils in a blender or food processor until it almost becomes a powder.

Combine powder and 1 Tablespoon oil to a frying pan and roast on medium heat for about two to three minutes, stirring constantly.

Turn off the heat. Add all the spice and two Tablespoons of warm water. Let sit for ten minutes and cover with a damp cloth.

To make the Kachoris
Knead dough and divide into 12 equal parts.

Flatten the edges of each and make into 3-inch circle. Mold the dough into a cup and place 1 teaspoon of filling in the center. Pull the edges of the dough to the center to close. Repeat with the rest.

Set the Kachoris on a surface with the seams facing up. Gently flatten the seams.

Heat 2 inches of oil in a frying pan over medium heat. To check if oil is ready put a little piece of dough in the oil, it should sizzle and come up slow.

Fry a few at a time. Turn when they begin to puff. Fry until golden-brown on both sides.

Papdi Chaat

Papdi Chaat is made of crispy wafers garnished with potatoes, chickpeas, seasoned yogurt, and flavorful spices and chutneys.

Serves 4

Papdi
1 cup Gluten-Free All-Purpose flour
1/4 cup chickpea flour
1 teaspoon Xanthan or Guar gum
2 Tablespoons oil
½ teaspoon salt
½ cup warm water

Garnish
Several small potatoes, peeled, boiled, and sliced
Cooked chickpeas, rinsed and drained
Plain vegan yogurt
Salt
Cumin
Red chili powder
Chutney of choice

To make Papdi
In a bowl mix flours, gum, salt and oil. Add the water a little at a time while kneading until it forms a dough. You may not need the entire amount. Cover and set aside for 30 minutes or more.

Divide the dough into 3 equal parts. Roll each section into a 6 inch round. Prick dough with a fork in several areas to prevent puffing while frying. Cut each round into squares, about 2 inches each, with a sharp, oiled knife.

Heat two inches of oil in a medium sized frying pan over medium heat. To check if the oil is ready, just put a small piece of dough in the oil. The dough should sizzle right away but come up to the surface slowly. If the dough rises immediately, lower the heat for a moment and try again.

Make sure to place just enough Papdi to cover top of the oil in the frying pan in a single layer. Fry until both sides are golden.

Remove and drain on paper towels. Papdi will take on a crispier texture as they cool.

Serving

Arrange the Papdi on a large plate. Place potatoes on top of each Papdi.

Mash the chickpeas coarsely (chunkier than hummus) and mix with chutney to your taste. Divide mixture and place an equal amount on top of the potato slices.

Dilute yogurt with a bit of milk to make a thin sauce. Add salt to taste. Drizzle yogurt over each Papdi.

Sprinkle with cumin powder, red chili powder, and any other spices to taste.

Sabudana Khichdi

This nutty Tapioca dish is traditionally served as an appetizer, but makes an equally delicious breakfast.

Serves

1½ cups tapioca pearls
½ cup sliced almonds or other nuts, optional
½ cup frozen green peas (canned are too mushy)
3 Tablespoons oil
½ teaspoon cumin seeds
¼ teaspoon turmeric
¼ teaspoon cinnamon
1 teaspoon salt
1 Tablespoon lemon juice

Gently wash then soak tapioca in about ½ cup of water 8 hours or overnight.

Heat the oil in a frying pan on medium heat. Add cumin seeds and peas and stir fry until peas are defrosted and hot.

Add the tapioca and stir fry for 3 to 4 minutes. Add turmeric, and salt and cook over medium heat, stirring frequently but gently, until tapioca changes in color, about 5-10 minutes.

Add nuts and lemon juice before serving.

Sabudana Vada

Tapioca dumpling filled with potatoes. For variety, you can add 1 cup shredded vegan cheese to the filling.

Makes 3 dozen

9 medium potatoes, peeled
1 cup tapioca
1 Tablespoon of salt
2 teaspoons cumin seeds
2 Tablespoons finely chopped cilantro
1 teaspoon lemon juice
Oil for frying

Wash the tapioca and soak in 9 cups of water for at least 4 hours or more. Drain.

Parboil the potatoes, making sure to not fully cook. To check, insert a knife or fork into each potato to make sure they are not fully cooked. Drain and cool. Grate potatoes when they are at room temperature.

Mix all the ingredients together. The dough should be a little sticky and soft.

Divide mixture into 36 portions.

Oil your hands. Roll each portion into a patty.

Heat two inches of oil in a frying pan over medium-high heat. To check if the oil is ready, drop a small piece of dough into the oil. The dough should rise to the surface, and not change its color immediately.

Slowly drop the patties into the frying pan. Do not cook too many at one time. Fry until both sides are golden brown, approximately 2-3 minutes. Flip over and continue to cook until evenly browned.

Drain on paper towels. Serve hot as is or with chutney.

Raja Sweet Potatoes

This is equally good with turnips, white potatoes, or beets.

Serves 8

8 medium sweet potatoes
2 Tablespoons lemon juice
1 teaspoon grated ginger *or* ½ teaspoon ground ginger
1 teaspoon salt
1 teaspoon black salt
1 teaspoon ground black pepper
1 teaspoon roasted ground cumin seed
1 teaspoon Curry powder
1 cup vegan cheddar cheese *or* crumbled Paneer

Boil the sweet potatoes until just done. Do not over boil.

Peel the skin and slice them into 1/8 inch thick pieces.

Mix all the spices with ginger and lemon juice.

Place the sweet potato slices over a plate.

Spread few drops of spice mix over every piece. Sprinkle cheese or Paneer on top,

Preheat oven to 350°F.

Grease a 9x13 baking dish. Assemble potatoes in pan, sprinkle with some cheese, and cover with a second layer of potatoes. Repeat.

Bake 15 minutes, or until cheese/Paneer is melted and bubbling.

Veggie Patties

These also make great burgers or sandwiches.

Makes 8

2 medium potatoes, peeled
1 cup frozen mixed vegetables, defrosted
1 teaspoon turmeric
1 teaspoon salt
3 Tablespoons chickpea flour
1 cup Gluten-Free breadcrumbs
Oil for frying

Wash and scrub the potatoes. Add to a pot and cover with water. Boil the potatoes until they are tender. Drain and cool.

Peel and mash the potatoes.

Mix all the ingredients together.

Add 4 Tablespoons of water to the flour to make a batter and set aside.

With oiled hands, divide the mixture into 8 equal parts. Shape into ½ inch thick patties. Dip each patty in the batter, then roll in breadcrumbs.

Heat two inches of oil on medium-high heat in a frying pan. To check if the oil is ready, put one drop of batter in the oil, the batter should come up right away.

Fry a few cutlets at a time to keep the oil from cooling. Cook until they are golden, about 3-5 minutes, flip, and cook on the other side.

Samosas

Samosas are probably the most popular Indian appetizer, and each region has their own recipe. I've chosen the Northern Indian Samosa recipe, which are my favorite.

Makes 2 dozen

Dough
1 cup Gluten-Free All-Purpose flour
½ cup plus 2 Tablespoons chickpea flour
1 teaspoon Xanthan or Guar gum
1 teaspoon salt
3 Tablespoons oil
2/3 cup warm water

Filling
9 large boiled potatoes, peeled and diced
1 teaspoon cumin seeds
2 teaspoon coriander powder
½ teaspoon Garam Masala
1 Tablespoon salt
¼ cup oil
1 cup green peas

Mix the flours, gum, salt, oil, and salt together to make a soft dough. Add water slowly, as you may not need all of it. Add more if needed. Knead 1-2 minutes.

Set the dough aside for at least 30 minutes and cover it with damp cloth.

Heat the oil in a frying pan over medium-high heat. Add cumin seeds and green peas and turn heat to medium, cooking 3-5 minutes or until peas become soft.

Add the potatoes and continue to cook for about 4 minutes. Stir in Garam Masala and coriander. Let the filling cool to room temperature.

To assemble Samosas
Take 2 Tablespoons of water and 1 Tablespoon of chickpea flour to make a paste and set aside.

Knead the dough for a minute.

Divide the dough into 4 equal parts and make into balls.

Roll each ball into 6-inch diameter circles and cut each circle in half.

Spread the paste lightly all along the edge of one. Fold it in half. Pinch the side to seal.

Fill with 3 Tablespoons of filling. Now close and shape into a triangle, pinching the top edge so that it is completely sealed.

Continue filling the rest of the Samosas in this way until done.

Heat 2 inches of the oil in a frying pan over medium heat. Do not allow oil to get too hot, as for this recipe, it will make them soggy. To check if oil is hot enough place a small piece of dough in oil and dough should sizzle and come to the surface slowly.

Place the Samosas in the frying pan a few at a time. Turn when they begin to float, and fry until they turn golden on both sides.

Breads

Naan

An Indian flatbread, much like pita, bit shaped more oblong, like a wrapper.

Makes 6

½ cup water
2 teaspoons granulated sweetener
2 teaspoons active dry yeast
2 cups brown rice flour
½ cup potato starch
½ teaspoon salt
1 teaspoon baking powder
1 teaspoon Xanthan or Guar gum
2 teaspoons vegetable oil
½ cup plain soy yogurt
Egg replacer for one egg, prepared according to instructions
Extra flour for flouring the surface

Preheat the oven to 450°F.

Place a heavy baking tray or pizza stone in the oven to heat while you prepare the ingredients.

In a measuring bowl or cup, mix water with 1 teaspoon of the sweetener and the yeast. Allow to sit in a warm place while you prep the rest of the ingredients.

Combine the flour, starch, salt, baking powder, and Xanthan in a medium bowl. Add the remaining sweetener, oil, yogurt, egg replacer, and the water/yeast mixture. Blend until smooth. It will be very thick.

Divide the dough into six equal portions. Sprinkle some flour onto your rolling surface or use your hands to press the dough into a pita shape. Roll the dough until it is about ¼" thick. Sprinkle more flour as needed onto the dough and/or the rolling pin to keep it from sticking.

When you are ready to bake, carefully place each piece of dough onto your baking pan or stone. Bake for 6 minutes, flip over and bake for another 4-6 minutes until they are very browned.

Paratha

Parathas are another style of Indian flatbread

Makes 12

Dough
1 cup chickpea flour
1 cup Gluten-Free All-Purpose flour
2 teaspoons Xanthan or Guar gum
1 cup of water
¼ teaspoon salt
½ cup of chickpea or other Gluten-Free flour for rolling
Oil for surface

Making Dough
Mix flours, gum, salt, and gradually add water to make soft dough. Add more water if needed. Knead the dough for a few minutes on a lightly greased surface.

Set dough aside and cover it with a damp cloth. Let the dough rest for at least 30 minutes.

Making Paratha
Divide the potato mixture and the dough into 12 equal parts. The potato balls should be almost twice the size as the dough balls.

Roll the dough into 3 inch circles. Place the potato balls in the center. Seal by pulling the edges of the rolled dough together to make a ball. Continue with until you have made all the Parathas.

Heat three inches of oil in a large heavy skillet on medium-high heat. Before frying, check the temperature of the oil by sprinkling a couple of drops of water in the pan. If the water sizzles right away, the oil is ready.

Roll each Paratha in flour. Roll each one into a 6-inch circle. Fry Parathas one at a time. After a few seconds you will see the Paratha change color and puff. When this happens, flip over. Continue to fry and flip again, lightly pressing any puffed areas with a spatula. Remove from oil and drain. Check oil temperature before proceeding to cook the rest.

Battura

Battura is fried puffed bread and is often served with chickpeas. This recipe makes a half dozen, but you can easily double or triple it if needed.

Makes 6

2 cups Gluten-Free All-Purpose flour
4 Tablespoons chickpea flour
2 teaspoons Xanthan or Guar gum
2 teaspoons active dry yeast
1 teaspoon any sweetener, such as agave nectar
1 teaspoon salt
3 Tablespoons plain vegan yogurt
2 Tablespoons oil
¾ cup warm water
Oil for frying
¼ cup flour for rolling

Dissolve yeast in water heated to 110°F or as directed on yeast package. Let it sit and dissolve for 10 minutes. It should turn foamy.

Combine flours, gum, sweetener, and salt in a separate bowl and mix well.

Next, add oil and yogurt to the flour. Stir well.

Add yeast mixture to the flour and make into soft dough. Add more water or flour as needed to get the right consistency.

Cover and allow to rise 3-4 hours. Dough should double in size.

Punch down dough and knead on floured surface. Divide the dough into 6 equal parts. Shape into balls and flatten with hands.

Heat two inches oil in a frying pan over high heat. To check if oil is hot enough place a small piece of dough in oil and dough should floats to top right away.

Place the Battura in the frying pan one at a time. Battura will puff and turn light brown quickly. Turn and allow it to brown on the other side. Remove and drain on paper towels. Check oil temperature before cooking the rest.

Puri

Puri is another version of a traditional Indian bread. That has only a few ingredients and is very simple to make.

Makes 8

1 cup chickpea flour
½ cup warm water
½ teaspoon salt
1 teaspoon oil
Oil for frying

Mix flour and salt. Add water as needed to make firm dough. You may not use all of the water.

Oil your hands and knead the dough. Puri dough should be firm.

Set the dough aside and cover with a damp cloth for 30 minutes or longer.

Divide the dough in 8 equal parts.

Roll each into 6 inch circles. If the dough is sticking, put couple of drops oil on the rolling pin and the counter. It is suggested you roll these one at a time as they can puff easily.

Heat two inches oil in a frying pan over high heat. To check if oil is hot enough place a small piece of dough in oil and dough should float to the top right away.

Place the Puri in the frying pan and press it with a spatula. Puri should puff right away. Once this happens, turn Puri over. Cook until it is a light golden color. Take the Puri out and place it on paper towels to absorb the excess oil.

Check oil before cooking the rest of the batch.

Chapati/Roti/Fulka

The same bread, with three different names, depending on the region. Whichever name you use, it is an Indian flat bread traditionally made with whole-wheat flour. It is served along with meals, as an appetizer, or can be used as a tortilla. Unlike the other featured breads, Chapati uses very little oil to prepare.

Makes 8

½ cup chickpea flour
½ cup Gluten-Free All-Purpose Flour
1 teaspoon Xanthan or Guar gum
¼ teaspoon salt
½ cup warm water
2 teaspoons vegan butter or coconut oil
¼ cup additional flour for rolling

Mix flours, salt, gum, and water together to make a soft dough. Stir in water gradually. Adjust if needed.

Knead the dough on a lightly oiled surface.

Set the dough aside and cover with a damp cloth. Let the dough rest for at least ten minutes or more.

Divide the dough into 8 equal parts. Roll into balls and flatten into a 6-inch circles. Dough may stick, so use a bit oil or flour as needed.

Heat a small skillet over medium-high heat, using a small amount oil or non-stick cooking spray. Place one chapatti at a time into the skillet.

After Chapati starts changing color and begins to puff, flip over. Cook for about 30 seconds, then flip again. Flatten with spatula and press lightly on the puffed parts. When it is golden on both sides, it is done.

Coat top with coconut oil or vegan butter.

Coat pan with another small amount oil or non-stick spray and continue to cook the rest of the batch.

Methi Thepla

Methi Thepla is a Gujarati snack bread flavored with Fenugreek leaves, hence the name. If you cannot find fenugreek leaves in your area, you can add 1 teaspoon fenugreek seeds and ¼ cup cilantro leaves instead.

Makes 6

1 cup Gluten-Free All-Purpose flour
¼ cup chickpea flour
1 teaspoon Xanthan or Guar gum
½ teaspoon cumin seeds
½ teaspoon turmeric
1 teaspoon salt
¼ cup dry fenugreek leaves
2 Tablespoons oil
¼ cup plain vegan yogurt
3 Tablespoons of water as needed
Oil for cooking

Mix all the dry ingredients together in a bowl and set aside.

Combine oil and yogurt together, blending well. Add the yogurt mixture to the dry ingredients and mix well. Add water as needed to make firm dough.

Knead the dough for 2 minutes on a lightly greased surface.

Cover dough with a damp cloth and let rise for at least 30 minutes.

After 30 minutes or more, divide the dough into 6 equal parts. Using your hands, roll each one into a smooth ball and press flat.

Take each ball and press it in some dry flour on both sides. Using a rolling pin roll each dough into 5 to 6" diameter circle. If dough starts sticking, dust it with a small amount of flour.

Cooking the Thepla
Heat the oil in a heavy skillet over medium-high heat. The oil is ready, when a couple of drops of water sizzle immediately.

Cook one at a time. Flip over when the color begins to change. Using a spatula, lightly press the entire Thepla.

Turn over again and press with the spatula, making sure it is golden on both sides. Remove from heat and drain on paper towels.

Check oil temperature before repeating with the remaining dough.

Pav Bhaji

Pav Bhaji are spicy buns. They are normally a little bit more work than some of the other breads, but if you use store bought Gluten-Free buns like I suggest, they are rather fast.

Serves 6

2 medium potatoes, peeled and diced
1 cup chopped cauliflower florets
½ cup frozen peas, defrosted
½ cup diced carrots
3 Tablespoons oil
3 Tablespoons vegan butter or coconut oil
½ teaspoon ground ginger
3 medium tomatoes, diced
½ teaspoon red chili
½ teaspoon turmeric
2 teaspoons salt
1 teaspoon Garam Masala
1 Tablespoon lemon juice
¼ cup chopped cilantro
6 Gluten-Free buns

Boil the vegetables, potatoes, and peas, in about 1 ½ cups of water. After the vegetables are tender, drain and mash.

Heat the oil in a frying pan over medium heat. Add tomatoes, cilantro, and ginger, red chili powder, fennel seed and turmeric, cooking for 2 minutes.

Add mashed vegetables. While cooking, mash the vegetable mix together for about 5 minutes. Add salt and butter or coconut oil, stir-fry for another minute.

Add about ¼ cup of water if needed and let it cook for a minute.

Remove from heat. Add Garam Masala, and lemon juice, mixing well.

Butter the buns and toast in a skillet over medium heat until buns are golden.

Remove buns and top with vegetable topping.

Soups and Salads

Saar

This is a traditional Tomato soup. Feel free to modify it by adding rice, Gluten-Free pasta, or even Paneer or vegan cheese at the very end.

Serves 4

8 large tomatoes
1 small can (8 ounces) tomato sauce
1 cup water
1 cup Mimic Crème, or other unsweetened milk product
2 Tablespoons coconut oil or vegan butter
1 teaspoon mustard seeds
1 teaspoon Curry powder
2 teaspoons agave nectar or other sweetener
1 teaspoon paprika
Salt and pepper to taste
2 Tablespoons chopped fresh cilantro

Place the tomatoes and 1 cup water in a microwave-safe bowl, and cook on High 4 minutes in the microwave. Reserve the cooking water. Cool tomatoes slightly, peel, and discard skins.

Process the tomatoes, water, and garlic in a blender or food processor until smooth.

Melt the butter or coconut oil in a skillet over medium heat, and cook the mustard seeds 1 minute. Stir in the Curry. Pour the tomatoes into the skillet.

Stir in the crème or milk product. Mix in sweetener, paprika, and salt. Bring to a boil, then quickly reduce heat to low. Simmer 10 minutes, and stir in cilantro just before serving.

Carrot Peach Soup

This is a surprisingly tasty soup, especially in the summer when tomatoes and peaches are in season.

Serves 4

1 Tablespoon oil
1 large onion, diced
5 medium carrots, chopped
2 peaches, peeled and sliced
1 fresh red chili pepper, chopped
3 (28 ounce) cans of tomatoes, including juice
1 cup vegetable stock
1 Tablespoon sweetener of choice
1 teaspoon curry powder
Salt and pepper to taste
1 cup Mimic Crème or other unflavored milk product

Heat the oil in a large skillet over medium heat, and cook the onions, carrots, and chili pepper until tender.

Mix in tomatoes, vegetable stock, curry, sweetener, and peaches. Season with salt and pepper. Bring to a boil. Reduce heat to low, and simmer 30 minutes.

Transfer the soup in batches to a blender or food processor, and blend until smooth. Return to the pot, and continue cooking until heated through. Mix in the crème or milk, and heat over medium heat. Remove from heat just before it begins to boil.

Broccoli & Cheddar Soup

What could be better than a creamy, spicy, cheddary bowl of soup on a snow day?

Serves 4

1 quart vegetable stock
2 medium potatoes, diced and peeled
2 heads of broccoli, finely chopped
1 teaspoon Garam Masala
1 teaspoon red chili
Salt and pepper to taste
¼ cup chickpea flour
½ cup Mimic Crème or other unflavored milk product
2 cups shredded vegan Cheddar cheese
1 can chickpeas, rinsed and drained

In a stockpot, combine stock, onion, potatoes, and broccoli. Bring to a boil and reduce heat to low. Continue to simmer until vegetables are tender. Season with Garam Masala powder, chili, salt, and pepper.

In a bowl, combine flour and the milk/crème. Whisk briskly until there are no lumps. Add mixture to soup, stirring continuously as soup thickens.

Pour half of the soup into blender or food processor. Blend until chunky. Return to the pot, and continue to cook another 10 minutes. Add chickpeas.

Stir in vegan cheddar just before serving.

Purple Salad

This dish earns its name by the color it turns. Full of nutrients, this is a quick and easy meal anytime.

Serves 4

1 Tablespoon oil
¼ teaspoon turmeric
2 cups plain vegan yogurt
1 teaspoon red chili powder
1 (15 ounce) can sliced beets, drained
1 cup red cabbage, shredded
1 can (15 ounces) red kidney beans, rinsed and drained
½ red onion, diced
Salt and pepper, to taste
A few sprigs of mint, for garnish

Shred cabbage and dice onions. Set aside. Rinse and drain beets. Add kidney beans. Place together in a large bowl.

Season yogurt with turmeric, salt, and pepper.

Gently stir yogurt into the vegetables.

Refrigerate at least 2 hours before serving.

Coconut Curry Rice Salad

This can be served over salad greens.

Serves 6

3 cups cooked basmati rice
1 package tempeh, sliced
1 Tablespoon Coconut oil
1 cup Unsweetened coconut milk
½ cup celery, sliced
¼ cup scallions, chopped
¼ cup chopped Green pepper
1 cup vegan sour cream
¼ cup vegan mayonnaise
3 Tablespoons peach *or* mango chutney
2 teaspoons Curry powder
Salt and Pepper, to taste
¼ cup shredded coconut

In a large bowl, combine unsweetened coconut milk, 1 teaspoon of curry, and tempeh to form a marinade. Let sit, refrigerated, for at least one hour.

In a separate bowl, combine the rice, celery, green onions, vegan sour cream, vegan mayonnaise, chutney, the remaining Curry, and salt. Mix well, cover and refrigerate until chilled.

Heat coconut oil in a skillet over medium heat. Remove tempeh from marinade, reserving the milk. Fry, using some of the milk to help prevent it from sticking until browned, about 5 minutes.

Remove rice from refrigerator. Slowly stir in the unsweetened coconut milk marinade until it gets really thick and creamy, but not soupy. You may not need all of the marinade.

Add tempeh. Refrigerate at least one hour before serving.

Ashram Fruit Salad

One of my spiritual teachers, Jyoti Chakrananda, is a chef as well as a teacher at her ashram. This is one of her signature dishes.

Serves 4

- 1 cup basmati rice
- 1 cup water
- 1 cup Unsweetened coconut milk
- 1 pound of extra firm tofu, drained, pressed, and cubed
- 2 cups plain vegan yogurt
- ½ cup lime juice
- 1 Tablespoon Curry powder
- ½ cup golden raisins
- ¼ cup shredded coconut
- ½ cup chopped walnuts
- 1 mango, diced

In a saucepan bring water and unsweetened coconut milk to a boil. Add rice and stir. Reduce heat, cover and simmer for 20 minutes; set aside.

Bring a large pot of water to a boil. Cook tofu for 3 minutes; drain, and set aside to cool.

In a bowl, blend yogurt with lime juice and Curry powder.

In a large mixing bowl, toss together raisins, coconut, mango, walnuts, rice, and tofu. Drizzle with yogurt dressing, and toss until well coated. Sweeten, if desired.

Tandoori Tofu Salad

You can also try this with sliced tempeh or Portabellas.

Serves 4

1 cup agave nectar
2 Tablespoons of yellow mustard
Tablespoon ground cumin
1 Tablespoon Curry powder
1 cup plain vegan yogurt
2 Tablespoons Garam Masala
2 teaspoons lemon juice
1 pound of extra firm tofu, drained, dressed, and sliced into matchsticks
¾ cup drained canned pineapple tidbits
8 cups mixed salad greens of choice
4 sprigs fresh mint
4 wedges of lime

In a small bowl, whisk together agave nectar, mustard, ground cumin, and Curry powder. Cover, and refrigerate until serving.

In a baking dish, whisk together yogurt, Garam Masala, and lemon juice. Place tofu sticks in the dish, and turn to coat. Cover, and refrigerate for at least 1 hour to marinade.

Preheat oven to 350°F.

Grease cookie sheet, and arrange tofu slices in a single layer. Bake 10 minutes, gently turn over, brush with marinade, and continue to bake for another 10 minutes. Remove and allow to cool, adding more marinade.

In a large bowl, toss salad greens with dressing. Divide salad among 4 plates. Top each with tofu, and garnish with mint and a lime wedge.

Sprouted Spinach Salad

For variety, you can steam the vegetables, then add the raisins at the last minute.

Serves 4

2 cups raw spinach leaves
2 cups grated carrots
½ cup bean sprouts
½ cup golden raisins
1 teaspoon sweetener of choice
1 Tablespoon lemon juice
1 Tablespoon shredded coconut
1 Tablespoon chopped cilantro
1 Tablespoon oil
1 teaspoon mustard seed
1 teaspoon red chili
Salt and pepper, to taste

In a large bowl, gently toss the spinach, carrots, sugar, lemon juice, coconut, raisins, and cilantro.

Heat the oil in a small saucepan over medium heat. Stir in the mustard seed, red chili, and sprouts. Cook just until sprouts begin to brown, about 3 minutes. Mix into the salad. Season with salt and pepper.

Cabbage & Chana Dahl

This is one of my favorite salads, as you can simply soak the lentils without needing to actually cook them. Perfect for those following a raw diet. Feel free to substitute any other bean, or add cubed tofu instead.

Serves 4

Salad
2 cups of very finely chopped cabbage
2 medium seeded and finely chopped tomatoes
1 cup chopped cucumber
1 shredded carrot
10 minced mint leaves
¼ cup yellow lentils or split peas

Dressing
1 Tablespoon olive oil
1 Tablespoon balsamic vinegar
1 Tablespoon lemon juice
1 teaspoon ground ginger
1 teaspoon salt
1 teaspoon sweetener of choice
½ teaspoon ground black pepper

Soak the lentils/peas for at least 2 hours in warm water. When ready, the lentils/peas should be soft. Drain.

Mix lentils/peas with the chopped vegetables.

Combine all ingredients for the dressing.

Mix the salad and dressing together and refrigerate for at least 30 minutes to marinade.

Lentil Vegetable Soup

Lentil soup is healthy and very satisfying dish. It's a great served with one of our breads, followed by a dessert such as Prasad.

Serves 4

    6 cups vegetable stock
    ½ cup brown lentils
    2 potatoes, peeled and diced
    1 medium yellow onion, chopped
    1 cup of carrots, diced
    1 cup of celery, sliced
    3 medium size tomatoes, coarsely diced
    1 teaspoon ground ginger
    1½ teaspoons salt
    ½ teaspoon turmeric
    ½ teaspoon black pepper
    ½ teaspoon cumin seed
    ½ teaspoon Garam Masala

Wash lentils and soak in 2 cups of water for 1 hour or longer. Once soaked, the lentils should double in size. Drain.

Heat 6 cups of stock in a large soup pot. Add lentils, salt, turmeric, cumin seed, Garam Masala, black pepper, ginger, carrots, celery, and tomatoes. Bring to a boil, then reduce heat.

Remove half of the soup and add to a blender or food processor. Blend until thick, and return to the pot.

Simmer soup for 40 minutes.

Mulligatawny

Mulligatawny is often considered Irish, but the word actually means Pepper Water in Indian.

Serves 4

½ cup chopped onion
2 stalks celery, chopped
1 carrot, diced
¼ cup vegan butter
2 Tablespoons chickpea flour
1½ teaspoons Curry powder
4 cups vegetable stock
¼ cup basmati rice
1 pound of extra firm tofu, drained, pressed, and cut into cubes
Salt and pepper, to taste
½ cup Mimic Crème or unflavored milk product, heated

Melt butter, and cook onions, celery, and carrots in a large soup pot for 3-5 minutes, or until onion begins to brown.

Add flour and Curry, and cook 5 minutes more.

Add vegetable stock, mix well, and bring to a boil. Simmer 30 minutes on low-medium heat.

Add apple, rice, tofu, salt, and pepper. Simmer 15-20 minutes more, or until rice is done.

Stir in crème/milk product, and simmer just until warm. Do not boil.

Side Dishes

Vegetable Bhaji

Bhaji is simply a dish of fried vegetables, so feel free to use what you have.

Serves 4

4 large potatoes, peeled and diced
1 cup cauliflower florets
1 carrot, sliced
1 cup fresh green beans, trimmed
½ cup frozen green peas
2 Tablespoons oil
1 large onion, chopped
1 teaspoon mustard seeds
1 clove of garlic, minced
2 teaspoons ginger root, minced root
1 teaspoon cumin
1 teaspoon Curry powder
1 teaspoon red chili powder
1 cup of Mimic Crème or other milk product

Place the potatoes, cauliflower, carrots, and peas into a bamboo steamer or microwave safe bowl and steam until desired texture.

Place the oil in a large skillet over medium heat. Cook and the onion until it turns golden, about 10 minutes.

Add the mustard seeds and cook until the seeds begin to pop, about 30 seconds, and then add the garlic and ginger. Cook and stir until the garlic begins to brown, about 1-2 minutes.

Stir in the cumin, Curry powder, and chili powder, and then add the partially cooked potatoes, cauliflower, carrot, and peas. Cook and stir until the vegetables are tender and coated with spices, about 30 minutes.

Reduce heat and stir in milk/crème. Simmer for 10 minutes. Serve with rice and bread.

Saag

Saag is a Curry with a combination of bitter and mild greens. Any combination of seasonal greens will work. I personally prefer spinach with turnip greens, which is what I offer here. I like to add quartered, peeled potatoes, which is optional.

Serves 4

½ cup vegan butter or coconut oil
2 teaspoons cumin seed
4 medium russet potatoes, peeled and quartered optional
1 green chili pepper, seeded and diced
2 cloves of garlic, minced
2 Tablespoons turmeric
1 pound chopped fresh turnip greens
1 pound chopped fresh spinach leaves
1 teaspoon cumin
1 teaspoon coriander
1 teaspoon salt
1 teaspoon black pepper

In a large skillet, melt butter or coconut oil over medium-high heat. Cook cumin seed, chili pepper, garlic, and turmeric until fragrant, about 2 minutes.

Add potatoes and reduce heat. Cook for 15 minutes, stirring frequently.

Stir in the greens and spinach a little at a time, until all greens have been added and begin to wilt.

Stir in the cumin, coriander, and salt and pepper. Cover; reduce heat and simmer until potatoes are tender, about 10 minutes, adding a small amount of water if needed.

Serve over basmati rice or Indian bread.

Squash and Spinach Curry

You could easily turn this into a main course by adding some beans, serving over rice, and rounding it out with a side of Naan.

Serves 4

¼ cup oil
1 large onion, chopped
2 Tablespoons Curry powder
2 cups unsweetened coconut milk
2/3 cup water
1 pound of kabocha, acorn, or other squash, peeled, and cut in large cubes
Salt and pepper to taste
1 (10 ounce) bag of fresh spinach leaves
1 Tablespoon fresh cilantro

Cook the onion in the oil over medium heat, until it begins to brown, about 5-10 minutes.

Stir in the Curry powder, and cook for 2 minutes longer.

Add the unsweetened coconut milk, water, and squash. Bring to a boil over high heat, then reduce heat to medium-low, cover, and simmer until the squash is tender, about 15-20 minutes.

Season to taste with salt and pepper, then stir in the spinach and cilantro. Simmer a few more minutes until spinach is wilted, and serve.

Roasted Eggplant

This is excellent served with basmati rice and red lentils.

Serves 4

2 pounds of eggplant
2/3 cup coconut oil or vegan butter
1 medium onion, chopped
4 large tomatoes, chopped
4 teaspoons crushed coriander seed
1 teaspoon turmeric

Preheat oven to 350°F.

Wash and peel the eggplant(s). Cut in half and bake for 20 minutes, or until very tender.

Remove from oven and cut eggplant into small pieces. The eggplant should be somewhat mushy and pulp-like.

Heat coconut oil or vegan butter in a skillet over medium heat. Cook onions until they begin to brown, about 5-7 minutes.

Stir in tomatoes, turmeric, crushed coriander, and eggplant; cook, stirring, until liquid evaporates

Remove from heat and serve.

Korma

The very first time I dined at an Indian restaurant, the staff recommended Korma. I have duplicated their recipe as best as I can, eliminating the heavy cream, reducing the oil, and of course, eliminating the chicken. You can add tofu or tempeh, but I find this dish is better without either.

Serves 4

2 Tablespoons coconut oil
1 large onion, diced
2 teaspoons ginger root, minced root
2 cloves of garlic, minced
4 large potatoes, peeled and cubed
4 carrots, cubed
1 jalapeno pepper, seeded and sliced, optional
1 (8 ounce) can tomato sauce
2 teaspoons salt
2 Tablespoons Curry powder
2 cups frozen green peas, defrosted
1 Green pepper, chopped
1 Red bell pepper, chopped
2 cups Mimic Crème or other milk product
1 teaspoon cilantro
1 teaspoon black pepper

Heat the oil in a large skillet over medium heat. Stir in the onion, and cook until tender, about 5-7 minutes. Mix in ginger and garlic, and continue cooking for an additional 1-2 minutes.

Add potatoes, carrots, jalapeno, cashews, and tomato sauce. Season with salt, pepper, cilantro, and Curry powder. Simmer for 15 minutes, or until potatoes are tender.

Stir in peas, peppers and crème/milk into the skillet. Reduce heat to low, cover, and simmer 10 minutes.

Peas and Mushrooms

For a special treat, I like to stir in 1cup Paneer or vegan shredded Mozzarella just before serving.

Serves

¼ cup coconut or other milk product
1 teaspoon red chili powder
2 teaspoons ground coriander seed
1 teaspoon turmeric
Salt and pepper, to taste
2 teaspoons ground ginger
1 large onion, chopped
½ teaspoon cinnamon
½ teaspoon cumin seeds
1 (15 ounce) can diced tomatoes, drained
1 pound fresh pea pods, shelled, or 16 ounces of frozen peas, defrosted
1 pound white button mushrooms, washed and sliced

In a small bowl, mix together unsweetened coconut milk, chili powder, coriander, turmeric, and salt. Set aside.

In a large skillet, heat oil over medium heat. Add onion, cinnamon, and cumin seeds. Cook until onions are soft, about 5-7 minutes.

Add mushrooms and continue to cook until soft, about 10 minutes.

Stir in tomatoes, peas, and unsweetened coconut milk mixture. Reduce heat, and simmer until the peas are tender if using fresh, or until warm if using frozen.

Potato Curry

I like to make this whenever I have leftover potatoes.

Serves 4

6 potatoes, peeled and cubed
3 Tablespoons coconut oil
1 large onion, diced
2 cloves garlic, minced
2 teaspoons ground cumin
½ teaspoon cayenne pepper
1 Tablespoon Curry powder
1 Tablespoon Garam Masala
1 teaspoon ground ginger
2 teaspoons salt
1 (15 ounce) can garbanzo beans (chickpeas), rinsed and drained
1 cup frozen green peas, defrosted
2 cups unsweetened unsweetened coconut milk

Place potatoes into a large pot and cover with water. Bring to a boil over high heat, then reduce to medium-low, cover, and simmer until tender, about 15 minutes. Do not over boil. Drain and remove from pan.

Heat the oil in a large skillet over medium heat. Stir in the onion and garlic and cook about 5 minutes. Season with cumin, cayenne pepper, Curry powder, Garam Masala, ginger, and salt; cook for 2 minutes more.

Add the garbanzo beans, peas, and potatoes. Pour in the unsweetened coconut milk, and bring to a simmer, 15-20 minutes or until the milk begins to evaporate and the mixture thickens.

Bengali Okra

I never used to like okra, until I tried it prepared this way. You can slice the okra, but it tends to create a sticky, almost slimy texture, so I prefer it whole and use the chickpea flour to reduce this in the dish.

Serves 4

1 pound fresh or frozen okra, ends trimmed
1 Tablespoon coconut oil
1 teaspoon whole cumin seeds
½ teaspoon Curry powder
½ teaspoon chickpea flour
Salt and pepper, to taste

Microwave the okra on High for 3 minutes or until just tender. You can also steam or gently boil the okra, but it tends to increase the natural stickiness.

Heat oil in a large skillet over medium heat. Add cumin seeds and cook until they begin to pop.

Add the okra. Cook for 5 minutes, then gently mix in the Curry powder, chickpea flour, and salt. Reduce heat and cook an additional 2 minutes more for the sauce to thicken. Serve immediately.

Potatoes Amchoor

You certainly can omit the mango powder, amchoor, if you have a hard time obtaining it, but that is what makes this dish unique. You could also simply top with our Pineapple-Mango chutney.

Serves 4

6 large russet potatoes, diced
1½ teaspoons cumin
1½ teaspoons ground coriander
1 teaspoon amchoor (dried mango powder)
½ teaspoon red chili powder, or to taste
1 teaspoon salt
3 Tablespoons oil
Vegan yogurt and cilantro, as garnishes

Place the potatoes into a large pot and cover water. Bring to a boil over high heat, then reduce heat to medium-low, cover, and simmer until tender, about 12 minutes. Drain.

Transfer into a bowl and sprinkle with cumin, coriander, amchoor, red chili powder, and salt. Toss gently to evenly coat the potatoes with the spices.

Garnish with cilantro and vegan yogurt.

Raisined Peppers

This unusual blend of ingredients blends amazingly well together. Feel free to add tofu, tempeh, or potatoes for more substance.

Serves 4

2 Tablespoons oil
½ green pepper, seeded and sliced into strips
1 Tablespoon fresh ginger root, minced
1 Tablespoon garlic, minced
1 teaspoon ground coriander
½ teaspoon red chili powder
¼ teaspoon turmeric
¼ teaspoon cumin seeds
A pinch of cinnamon
1 small tomato, sliced
¼ cup golden raisins
1 cup sliced okra
1 cup unsweetened coconut milk
1 Tablespoon water
Salt and pepper, to taste

Heat the oil in a large skillet and cook the pepper for about 3 minutes. Stir in the ginger, garlic and cook until fragrant, about 2 to 3 minutes more.

Season with coriander, red chili powder, turmeric, cumin seeds, salt, black pepper, and cinnamon; cook another 2 minutes.

Add the tomato and raisins to the mixture, continuing to cook 3 more minutes. Mix the okra in gently.

Stir the unsweetened coconut milk and water together in a small bowl and add to the mixture.

Cover and cook until the okra is tender, about 8 to 10 minutes. Add water if needed to keep moist.

Aloo Gobi

This delicious meal makes such a beautiful presentation, that I almost chose its photo for the book cover. However, since many of my Facebook friends thought it was General's Chicken, so I went for the Indian Butter Tofu instead.

Serves 4

¼ cup coconut oil
1 medium onion, chopped
1 Tablespoon garlic, minced
1 teaspoon cumin
1 (15 ounce) can diced tomatoes
1 (8 ounce can) tomato sauce
2 cups (coconut) milk or Mimic Crème
1 Tablespoon salt
1 Tablespoon turmeric
1 Tablespoon chili powder
1 teaspoon ground ginger
3 large potatoes, peeled and cubed
1 large head of cauliflower, chopped into bite sized florets
1 (15 ounce) can garbanzo beans, rinsed and drained
2 Tablespoons Garam Masala

Heat oil in a large skillet over medium-high heat and add onion, cooking until softened, about 4 minutes. Stir in garlic and cumin, and continue to cook until onion begins to brown.

Stir in tomatoes, coconut milk, coriander, salt, turmeric, red chili powder, cinnamon, and ginger. Bring to a boil, then add potatoes, cauliflower, and garbanzo beans. Stir well, reduce heat to low and cover, simmering 30-45 minutes or until potatoes are tender.

Sprinkle in the Garam Masala, stir, and cook for an additional 5 minutes.

Vegetable Koftas

Koftas are dumplings or croquettes simmered in a delicious gravy. This also makes a great main course for two served over rice or Biryani.

Serves 4

For the Koftas
1½ cups frozen mixed vegetables, thawed
2 slices Gluten-Free bread
1¼ cups mashed potatoes
1 medium onion, chopped fine
1 teaspoon fresh ginger root, minced
1 teaspoon salt
Oil, for frying

For the Gravy
2 Tablespoons vegan butter
2 medium onions, chopped
1 teaspoon ginger root, minced
2 garlic cloves, minced
2 teaspoons ground coriander
½ teaspoon turmeric
½ teaspoon Garam Masala
½ cup tomato paste
1 cup Mimic Crème or coconut milk
Salt and pepper, to taste

Boil the mixed vegetables till soft. Drain, and allow to cool to room temperature. When cool, chop fine by hand or briefly in a food processor and set aside.

Moisten the slices of bread with a little water to create a doughy substance. Combine this with the vegetables, mashed potatoes, onion, ginger, and salt. Form into 8 balls.

Heat four inches of oil in a deep heavy skillet or prepare a deep fryer for 375°F. Oil is ready when a drop of water immediately sizzles.

Fry the Koftas, just 2 at a time, until golden brown. Drain on paper towels, and allow to cool.

Make the gravy by melting the butter in a large saucepan over medium-high heat. Stir in the onions, ginger, garlic, coriander, turmeric, and Garam Masala and cook until the onions have softened.

Mix in the tomato paste and cook for 5 minutes. Pour in the milk or crème and season with salt and pepper, cooking an additional 10-15 minutes more to thicken, stirring frequently.

To serve, add Koftas in the gravy and simmer for a few minutes.

Creamy Coconut Cabbage

I have also really enjoyed this dish with cauliflower instead of cabbage.

Serves 4

2 Tablespoons coconut oil
2 Tablespoons vegan butter
1 small onion, thinly sliced
1 cup carrots, cut into thin strips
1 clove garlic, minced
1 small head cabbage, thickly shredded
¼ cup shredded coconut
2 Tablespoons Curry powder
¾ cup unsweetened coconut milk
Salt and pepper to taste
1 medium tomato, deiced
¼ cup chopped scallions, both green and white parts

Heat the oil in a large skillet and fry the onion, carrot, and garlic until the onion begins to soften, about 3 minutes.

Add the cabbage, shredded coconut, and Curry powder and stir fry for 2 minutes.

Reduce heat to medium-low and add the coconut milk, salt, and pepper.

Cover, and cook to desired doneness. Stir in scallions and tomatoes during the last minute of cooking.

Aviyal

Aviyal is a customary southern Indian recipe that is frequently passed down from mother to daughter. Jyoti Chakrananda was kind enough to share her family's recipe with me here.

Serves 4

½ cup shredded coconut
1 Tablespoon coriander seeds
¼ cup red lentils
1 teaspoon cumin seeds
2 green chili peppers, chopped and seeded
2 cups plain vegan yogurt
1 cup vegetable stock
½ cup fresh green beans, cut
2 medium potatoes, peeled and cubed
1 medium tomato, diced
½ cup diced carrot
½ cup diced green pepper
2 Tablespoons oil
1 teaspoon cumin seeds
1 teaspoon mustard seeds
½ teaspoon Curry Powder
¼ teaspoon red chili powder

Place the coconut, coriander seeds, cumin seeds, and lentils in a container and cover with water. Soak for 2 hours. Drain.

Grind the mixture in a coffee grinder, food processor, or mortar and pestle with the green chili peppers until it turns into a thick paste. Stir in the yogurt and set aside.

Add the stock and salt to a large pot and bring to a boil Reduce heat to medium and add the green beans, potatoes, and carrot to the water and cook until tender. Reduce heat to low and stir the yogurt and green peppers, and simmer for 5 minutes.

Heat the oil in a small skillet. Fry the cumin seeds and mustard seeds until they begin to pop. Add the Curry powder, tomato, and red chili powder to the mixture and fry together another 30 seconds. Stir the mixture into the vegetable mixture and serve.

Aloo Phujia

This spicy potato dish can also double as a breakfast on a cold winter morning.

Serves 4

1 medium onion, chopped
¼ cup oil
1 pound of potatoes, peeled and cubed
1 teaspoon salt
½ teaspoon black pepper
¼ teaspoon ground ginger
¼ teaspoon red chili powder
½ teaspoon ground turmeric
½ teaspoon Garam Masala
2 large tomatoes, diced

Heat oil in a medium skillet over medium heat. Add onion and all spices, cooking for 7-10 minutes, until browned.

Stir in potatoes, reduce heat to medium-low, and cover, simmering 15 minutes, stirring frequently.

Add tomatoes, cover pan once again and cook until potatoes are soft, about 10 minutes more.

Eggplant Punjab

Serves 4

1 pound of eggplant, peeled and halved
2 Tablespoons oil
½ teaspoon cumin seeds
1 medium onion, diced
1 teaspoon minced fresh ginger
1 large tomato, diced
1 clove garlic, minced
½ teaspoon turmeric
½ teaspoon ground cumin
¼ teaspoon red chili powder
Salt and pepper, to taste

Preheat the oven to the Broil setting.

Coat the eggplant with oil and place under the broiler, cooking until the flesh begins to soften, about 10 minutes, then turn over and repeat. When done remove from oven and allow to cool.

Once it is cool enough to touch, chop up the flesh and set aside.

Heat the oil in a large skillet over medium-high heat. Add the cumin seeds and let them cook until they begin to pop.

Add onion, ginger, and garlic and cook for 5 minutes.

Stir in the tomato, and season with turmeric, ground cumin, red chili powder, salt, and pepper. Cook and stir for a few minutes until the tomato begins to dissolve.

Add the eggplant to the skillet, and cook for 10 to 15 minutes or until most of the moisture evaporates.

Guferati

This is a wonderful way to serve fresh green beans and is a welcomed change on the holidays from the traditional green bean casserole.

Serves 4

1 pound fresh green beans, trimmed
1 Tablespoons coconut oil
1 Tablespoon mustard seeds
2 cloves of garlic, minced
½ teaspoon red chili pepper, crushed
1 teaspoon salt
½ teaspoon black pepper

Bring a large pot of water to a boil. Place the green beans in the pot, and boil for only 2-3 minutes. Green beans should still be firm and retain their green color. Drain, and immediately rinse with cold water.

Heat the oil in a skillet over medium heat and stir in the mustard seeds and garlic, cooking until the seeds begin to pop.

Add the chili powder and return the green beans to the skillet. Add salt and pepper

Cook for 8 minutes, stirring frequently or until tenderness is achieved.

Main Courses

Tempeh Curry

You can add any additional vegetables you have to this curry to make it into an Indian Stew.

Serves 4

1 pound of tempeh, sliced
2 medium onions, chopped
½ cup fresh or frozen green peas
2 teaspoons of Curry Powder
1 teaspoon of cornstarch or other starch
1 green pepper, chopped
4 Tablespoons coconut oil
2 Teaspoons ground ginger
1 teaspoon red chili powder
1 cup coconut milk
Tablespoon Garam Masala
¼ teaspoon turmeric
Salt and pepper to taste

Slice tempeh and marinade in coconut milk and Curry powder. Set aside for at least 30 minutes.

In a large skillet, sauté onions and green peppers in oil until they begin to brown.

Stir starch into marinade liquid. Remove tempeh but reserve liquid.

Add ginger and tempeh to the pan, cooking another 5 minutes, or until the tempeh begins to brown.

Add peas, Garam Masala, turmeric, red chili powder, and salt and pepper, and the marinade to the pan. Cover skillet and let simmer about 10 minutes, or until the milk has thickened into a gravy.

Serve with Biryani or basmati rice.

Tofu Keema

Freezing tofu after pressing and draining it really changes the texture. Try it and you may be quite surprised.

Serves 4

1 pound of extra firm tofu
3 Tablespoons oil
1 teaspoon cumin seeds
1 medium onion, chopped
1 teaspoon minced fresh ginger root
1 garlic clove, minced
1 cup frozen green peas, thawed
2 teaspoons Curry powder
1 large tomato, diced
Salt and pepper, to taste
1 fresh green chili pepper, diced

Drain tofu and wrap in towels. Place a heavy weight, such as a pan or large heavy can. Let press for at least 30 minutes. Remove the towels, wrap in plastic weap, and place in the freezer for at least 8 hours.

When ready, remove tofu from freezer, and defrost and dice.

Heat oil in a large skillet over medium heat. Add cumin seeds and cook until the seeds begin to pop. Add onion, ginger, and garlic and cook until browned.

Stir in tofu, peas, and Curry powder; cook, stirring frequently, for 5 minutes.

Add tomatoes, salt, and pepper. Cover, and cook for 15 minutes. Stir in chili pepper, and cook for and additional 2 to 3 minutes.

Baked Tofu Fillets

This is a rich Indian dish that is a great holiday meal. I especially like to serve this with Curry Potatoes.

Serves 4

    2 Tablespoons plain vegan yogurt
    1 teaspoon ground ginger
    2 teaspoons tomato paste
    1 teaspoon wheat-free tamari
    1 teaspoon balsamic vinegar
    5 Tablespoons lemon juice
    1 Tablespoon red chili powder
    2 Tablespoons ground coriander
    2 Tablespoons ground cumin
    1 teaspoon ground turmeric
    Salt and pepper, to taste
    1 pound of extra firm tofu, pressed and drained
    2 teaspoons vegan butter
    2 Tablespoons oil

Mix together in a large bowl the yogurt, ginger, garlic, tomato paste, tamari, vinegar, lemon juice, red chili powder, coriander, cumin, turmeric, salt and pepper. Place the tofu fillets into the marinade and flip over gently with a spatula to coat each side. Cover bowl and refrigerate for at least an hour.

Preheat oven to 400°F.

Use one teaspoon each of the vegan butter and oil to coat a shallow baking dish.

Remove the tofu from the marinade and place in baking dish. Drizzle with remaining oil and dot with the remaining butter. Bake until golden brown on top, about 30 to 40 minutes.

Bombay Noodles

I'm Italian and just had to create an Indian pasta dish ☺

Serves 8

1 (16 ounce) package Gluten-Free fettuccine or other similar pasta
3 Tablespoons coconut oil
1 teaspoon cumin seeds
1 large onion, chopped
2 cloves of garlic, minced
2 Portabella mushroom caps, sliced
2 Tablespoons Curry powder, divided
3 large tomatoes, diced
2 Tablespoons tomato paste
½ cup Mimic Crème or other milk product
1 teaspoon cornstarch or other starch

Bring a large pot of water to a boil and add the fettuccine. Return to a boil. Cook uncovered, stirring regularly, according to package instructions.

Heat the oil in a large skillet over medium-high heat. Fry the cumin seeds until they begin to pop, about 2 to 3 minutes.

Add the onion and garlic until lightly browned, about 5 minutes. Add the Portabellas and continue cooking until they begin to soften and shrink, about 5 minutes.

Add the Curry powder and the diced tomatoes and reduce heat to low. Stir in the tomato paste and simmer 15 minutes.

Stir the cooked pasta directly into the sauce to coat. Simmer 2 to 5 minutes, until pasta is reheated.

Bengali Stew

You can use just about any combination of vegetables in this stew. For convenience, you can make this in the microwave or on stove top. Both sets of instruction appear below.

Serves 4

1 medium onion, chopped
4 medium russet potatoes, peeled and diced
1 cup halved baby carrots
1 large tomato, diced
1 cup frozen green peas
8 ounces sliced button mushrooms
1 cup unsweetened coconut milk
1 cup vegetable broth
1 Tablespoon cumin
1 Tablespoon Curry powder
Salt and pepper to taste
¼ teaspoon red chili powder

Microwave instructions
Put all ingredients in a large microwave-safe bowl and mix thoroughly. Cover tightly and microwave on high for 20 minutes.

Stove top instructions
Add all ingredients to a large pot and simmer 35-40 minutes, or until the potatoes are tender but not mushy.

Sweet Vegetable Stew

This is a stew that is baked most of the way through, so it really becomes flavorful.

Serves

3 Tablespoons oil
1 (3 inch) piece of fresh ginger root, peeled and diced
2 cloves of garlic, minced
2 medium onions, peeled and diced
2 celery ribs, chopped
2 Tablespoons Curry powder
2 teaspoons coriander powder
1 teaspoon Garam Masala
1 teaspoon ground turmeric
2 carrots, peeled and diced
2 parsnips, peeled and diced
2 potatoes, peeled and cubed
2 apples - peeled, cored and chopped
1 cup raisins
1 cup cashews
½ cup Mimic Crème or other milk product

Preheat oven to 350°F. Grease a 9x13 baking dish or line with foil.

Heat the oil in a large stock pot over medium-high heat. Stir in the ginger, garlic, onions, and celery, and cook until vegetables soften, about 5 minutes.

Mix in the Curry powder, coriander powder, Garam Masala, and turmeric. Cook 5 minutes and stir in the carrots, parsnips, potatoes, and apples, raisins, and cashews, and toss to evenly blend the spices.

Pour the mixture into prepared roasting pan. Pour the milk product over the mixture. Cover and bake until the vegetables are soft, about 1 hour.

Mussaman Curry

This is a good winter dish you can make in a crock pot.

Serves 4

2 potatoes, cut into large chunks
1 small onion, coarsely chopped
2 Tablespoons vegan butter
8 ounces of button mushrooms, sliced
1 pound of tempeh, cubed
2 cloves of garlic, minced
2 cups unsweetened coconut milk
¼ cup peanut butter
3 Tablespoons Curry powder
3 Tablespoons wheat-free Tamari
3 Tablespoons vegan brown sugar or other sweetener of choice
2 cups vegetable stock
½ cup unsalted, dry-roasted peanuts

Place the potatoes and onion in a crock pot.

Melt the butter in a skillet over medium-high heat. Cook the tempeh, onion, mushrooms, and garlic until the onions begin to brown on all sides, about 5-7 minutes.

Transfer the tempeh and garlic to the crock pot.

Return the skillet to the medium-high heat. Stir in the coconut milk, peanut butter, and Curry powder and cook until the peanut butter melts.

Pour the milk mixture into the crock pot. Turn on the Low setting and stir in the Tamari, brown sugar/sweetener, and vegetable stock into.

Cook on Low until the potatoes are fork-tender, about 4 to 6 hours. Stir the peanuts just before serving.

Beans and Turnips Masala

You can use any type of beans and substitute white or sweet potatoes for the turnips

Serves 4

    2 turnips, peeled and cubed
    1 cup water
    ½ teaspoon salt
    1 (14.5 ounce) can of chickpeas or any other beans, rinsed and drained
    3 Tablespoons oil
    ½ teaspoon cumin seeds
    ½ teaspoon fennel seeds
    1 small red onion, diced
    ½ teaspoon minced fresh ginger root
    1 clove of garlic, minced
    2 large tomatoes, diced
    ½ teaspoon black salt
    ½ teaspoon turmeric
    ½ teaspoon ground ginger
    2 Tablespoons Mimic Crème or other milk product
    1 teaspoon Garam Masala

Place turnips in a saucepan with enough water to cover. Bring to a boil over high heat, then reduce heat to medium-low, cover, and simmer until the turnips become soft, about 5 minutes.

Once tender, add the beans, and cook 5 minutes more. Drain and set aside.

Meanwhile, heat the oil in a skillet over medium-high heat. Stir in the cumin and fennel, and cook until the spices roast about 1-2 minutes.

Stir in the onion, and cook until it softens, about 5 minutes. Stir in the ginger, garlic, tomatoes, and salt, and continue cooking until the mixture thickens. Finally, stir in the turmeric, and milk/crème. Cook 2 minutes more.

Add the turnips and beans to the skillet and simmer 10 minutes. Season with Garam Masala before serving.

Biryani

For Biryani, long grain basmati rice is best.

Serves 4

4 Tablespoons coconut oil or vegan butter
4 small potatoes, peeled and cut in quarters
2 large onions, finely chopped
1 Tablespoon minced fresh ginger root
½ teaspoon red chili powder
½ teaspoon black pepper
1 teaspoon turmeric
1 teaspoon ground cumin
1 teaspoon salt
2 medium tomatoes, peeled and diced
2 Tablespoons plain vegan yogurt
1 Tablespoon chopped fresh mint leaves
¼ teaspoon ground cardamom
¼ teaspoon cinnamon
1 pound of Portabella mushrooms, sliced
2 Tablespoons oil
¼ teaspoon ground cloves
1 cup of basmati rice
4 cups vegetable stock

In a large skillet, use 2 Tablespoons of the butter or oil fry the potatoes until brown. Remove potatoes and set aside.

Add remaining butter or oil to the skillet and fry onion, mushrooms, garlic, and ginger until onion is soft. Add red chili powder, pepper, turmeric, cumin, salt, cardamom, and tomatoes. Fry and stir frequently for 5 minutes.

Add yogurt, mint, cardamom, and cinnamon. Cover and cook over low heat, stirring occasionally until the tomatoes reduce to a pulp. You can add some water, milk/crème, or stock if needed to prevent sticking.

In a medium-size pot, heat the vegetable stock to a boil. When it begins to boil, add the rice, mushroom mixture, and the potatoes. Bring to boil, then cover and reduce heat to low and simmer for 20 minutes. Do not lift lid or stir while cooking. Biryani is done when rice is soft and the stock is evaporated.

Makhani Tofu (Indian Butter Tofu)

This is a special treat I like to bring for potlucks and other gatherings.

Serves 4

2 pounds of extra firm tofu, pressed, drained, and cubed

Marinade
1 Tablespoon lemon juice
1 Tablespoon red chili powder
Salt to taste
1 cup plain vegan yogurt
1 clove of garlic, minced
2 teaspoons Garam Masala
2 Tablespoons melted vegan butter
1 Tablespoon red chili powder
2 Tablespoons fresh minced ginger root

Sauce
2 Tablespoons lemon juice
2 Tablespoons oil
1 Tablespoon vegan butter
1 Tablespoon Garam Masala
1 Tablespoon fresh minced ginger root
1 clove of garlic, minced
2 cups tomato puree
1 teaspoon red chili powder
Salt and pepper, to taste
1 cup water
1 Tablespoon agave nectar or other sweetener
1 cup Mimic Crème or other milk product

To Marinade
Place tofu in a glass dish or bowl with lemon juice, 1 Tablespoon red chili powder and salt. Toss to coat; cover dish and refrigerate to marinate for at least 1 hour.

Drain yogurt in a cheesecloth or piece of muslin for 15 minutes. Transfer yogurt to a medium bowl and mix in salt, garlic, Garam Masala, vegan butter, red chili powder, ginger, lemon juice, and oil. Pour yogurt mixture over tofu, replace cover and refrigerate to marinate for another 4 hours or more hours.

Preheat oven to 400°F.

To Make Sauce
Melt vegan butter in a medium saucepan over medium heat. Stir in Garam Masala. When masala begins to pop, mix in ginger, garlic, and green chili peppers. Cook until tender, then stir in tomato puree, salt, pepper, and water. Bring to a boil; reduce heat to low and simmer, stirring in agave and crème/milk and turning off heat.

Place tofu on skewers. Place skewers in a 9x13 inch baking dish and bake for 15 minutes.

Remove baking pan from oven. Brush sauce over each skewer, then pour remainder over them equally. Continue to for another 5 minutes.

Tandoori Tempeh

Tempeh works well in this traditional chicken dish, but you can use Portabellas, tofu, or even thickly sliced potatoes instead.

Serves 4

1 ½ cups plain vegan yogurt
2 teaspoons salt
1 teaspoon black pepper
½ teaspoon ground cloves
2 Tablespoons fresh minced ginger root
1 clove of garlic, minced
1 Tablespoon paprika
2 teaspoons ground cumin
1 teaspoon cinnamon
2 teaspoons ground coriander
2 packages of tempeh, sliced

In a medium bowl, stir together yogurt, salt, pepper, cloves, and ginger. Mix in garlic, paprika, cumin, cinnamon, and coriander. Set aside.

Slice tempeh and place in a bowl or container. Pour yogurt mixture over tempeh, stir carefully, and cover. Refrigerate 8 hours, or overnight.

Preheat oven to 400°F. Grease a 9x13 baking dish with non-stick spray or oil.

Remove tempeh from refrigerator and discard marinade.

Place tempeh in the baking pan and cover with aluminum. Bake 30 minutes.

Green Bean Curry

Simple to make and really goes well with any soup or salad.

Serves 4

2 Tablespoons oil
1 teaspoon cumin seed
1 cup fresh green beans, trimmed and cut
2 medium onions, finely chopped
1 teaspoon turmeric
1 teaspoon red chili powder
1 teaspoon Garam Masala
1 clove garlic, minced
1 Tablespoon fresh ginger root, minced
5 large tomatoes, peeled, seeded, and diced
1 pound of extra firm tofu, drained, pressed, and cubed

Heat oil in a large saucepan over medium heat. Stir in cumin seed and cook until they start to pop, 20 to 45 seconds.

Stir in onion, and cook until golden brown, about 5 minutes. Season with turmeric, red chili powder, Garam Masala, garlic, and ginger. Cook for 1 to 2 minutes, or until they begin to brown.

Puree the tomatoes in a food processor or blender until smooth. Add the puree to the saucepan, and add the green beans.

Simmer gently until the green beans turn vibrant green but are still somewhat firm, has cooked, about 10 minutes. Add the tofu, and simmer for an additional 10 minutes. If needed, add water to prevent sticking.

Spinach Dahl

An Indian staple, Dahl (lentils) appears in many forms on Indian menus.

Serves 4

1½ cups brown lentils
3½ cups vegetable stock
½ teaspoon salt
1 teaspoon turmeric
¼ teaspoon red chili powder
1 pound fresh spinach, including stems, cleaned and trimmed
2 Tablespoons vegan butter
1 medium onion, chopped
1 teaspoon ground cumin
½ teaspoon mustard seed
1 teaspoon Garam Masala
½ cup unsweetened coconut milk

Rinse lentils and soak for 20 minutes.

In a large saucepan, bring water to a stock and add salt, lentils, turmeric and red chili powder. Cover and return to a boil, then reduce heat to low and simmer for 15 minutes.

Stir in the spinach and cook 5 minutes, or until lentils are soft. Add more stock if necessary.

In a small saucepan over medium heat, melt butter and cook onions with cumin and mustard seeds, stirring often. Cook until onions are soft, then add to the lentils. Stir in Garam Masala and unsweetened coconut milk and cook until heated through and the liquid has evaporated.

Dahl Kootu

Another traditional lentil dish, this one is most commonly made with red lentils, but you can use any type that you wish.

Serves 4

1 cup red lentils
½ cup yellow split peas
2 cups vegetable stock
2 Tablespoons oil
1 teaspoon mustard seed
1 carrot, peeled and diced
¼ cup frozen peas, thawed
½ teaspoon turmeric
1 teaspoon Curry powder
¼ teaspoon red chili powder
Salt and pepper, to taste
¼ cup shredded coconut

Bring the lentils, peas, and water to a boil in a saucepan. Reduce heat to medium-low, cover, and simmer until the peas are tender, about 30 minutes. Add more water if needed.

Heat the oil in a large skillet over medium heat. Stir in the mustard seeds, and cook until they begin to pop, about 2 minutes.

Stir in the Curry powder and the carrots, and cook for 5 minutes.

Add the peas, turmeric, red chili powder, peas, and salt and pepper. Cook until the vegetables have softened, about 5 minutes. Stir in the coconut just before serving.

Potatoes Calcutta

For variety, use equal amounts of russet and sweet potatoes.

Serves 4

3 Tablespoons coconut oil
2 pounds of potatoes, peeled (if desired) and diced
2 ½ cups cauliflower florets
1 large onion, sliced
2 cloves of garlic, minced
1 Tablespoon Curry powder
2 teaspoons ground ginger
½ cup red lentils, dry
3 large tomatoes, diced
1 cup vegetable stock
2 Tablespoons wheat-free Tamari
Salt and pepper, to taste

Heat oil in a large skillet over medium heat. Stir in potatoes, cauliflower, onion, and garlic and cook until the potatoes begins to brown, about 10 minutes.

Stir in the Curry powder and ginger, lentils, tomatoes, vegetable stock, Tamari, salt and pepper.

Cover, and simmer, stirring occasionally, until the lentils are tender, about 20 minutes.

Chickpea (Chana) Masala

No Indian cookbook is complete without a Chana Masala recipe.

Serves 4

2 Tablespoons coconut oil
1 clove of garlic, minced
½ cup onion, chopped finely
1 Tablespoon minced fresh ginger root
1 teaspoon Garam Masala
1 teaspoon Curry powder
¼ teaspoon red chili powder
1 large tomato, diced
1 ½ cups coconut milk or Mimic Crème
2 (15.5 ounce) cans chickpeas, drained and rinsed
Salt and pepper, to taste to taste

Heat oil in a saucepan over medium-high heat. Stir in the garlic, onion, and ginger, and cook until browned.

Stir in the Garam Masala, Curry, tomato, milk/crème, and chickpeas. Season to taste with salt and pepper.

Bring to a simmer, the reduce heat to low, simmering until garbanzos are very soft, about 20 minutes.

Desserts & Beverages

Burfi

Burfi is best described as a sweet, nutty candy, almost like peanut brittle. If you have allergies to any nuts, feel free to substitute any other nut, or soy nuts. For best results, you should use real vegan sugar and not a substitute and have a candy thermometer ready.

Makes 48 pieces

1 cup almonds, plain or flavored, if desired
1 cup walnuts
1 cup cashews
2½ cups vegan sugar*
1 cup water
1 teaspoon cardamom powder

Dry grind the walnuts, cashews and almonds in a food processor.

Toast in a frying pan over low-medium heat, for 5 minutes. Remove from heat and set aside.

Put the sugar and water together in a saucepan on medium heat. Bring to a boil to make a syrup. Cook until temperature reaches 230°F.

Remove from heat and stir in the cardamom powder.

Add the nuts to the syrup and mix, stirring vigorously, then spread over a greased cookie sheet. Do this quickly, as the mixture will harden as it cools.

Let the candy sit about 5 minutes, then cut into shapes. You can also allow Burfi to fully cool for one hour and allow it to make naturally. Allow cut Burfi to cool for about an hour before serving.

Reminder- in case you missed our mention in the Introduction, white sugar is not vegan, as it is processed with animal bones. Try to find sugar labeled vegan.

Apple Crumb

This Apple Crumb Pie is simple, delicious, and easy to make. If you are concerned about using gluten-free oats, you can substitute quinoa flakes.

Serves 4

    3 large Granny Smith Apples peeled, and sliced
    ¾ cup Gluten-Free oats or Quinoa flakes
    ¼ cup ground walnuts, almonds, or other nuts of choice, optional
    ½ cup agave or any other liquid sweetener *or* ¾ cup granulated sweetener
    1 teaspoon cinnamon
    ¼ teaspoon cardamom powder
    ½ cup vegan butter or coconut oil, divided into (2) ¼ cup portions

Preheat the oven 375°F.

In a bowl mix oatmeal/quinoa, walnuts, cinnamon, cardamom, sweetener, and butter/coconut oil. Set aside.

Arrange the apples evenly in a greased 9-inch pie plate.

Spread the oatmeal mix evenly over the apples. Take the second portion of butter or coconut oil and dot it on top.

Bake for 30 minutes on the center rack, turning once halfway through, and basting it in its juices.

Serve hot alone or topped with ice cream and a cup of chai.

Boondi

Boondis are small, mini donuts holes, served in a syrup. For best results, use a candy thermometer for the syrup.

Makes 8

3 cups chickpea flour
1½ cups of water, for Boondi
3 cups vegan sugar
½ cups water, for syrup
2 Tablespoons sliced almonds
1 pinch of cardamom powder
1 teaspoon cinnamon
Oil for frying

Put the water and sugar in a saucepan and bring to a boil on medium-high heat. When the syrup comes to a boil, turn the heat down to medium and stir to dissolve the sugar. Let it simmer until the syrup is 230°F according to the thermometer.

Mix the flour, cinnamon, and cardamom powder with water to make a smooth pancake-like batter. Set aside.

Heat two inches of oil in a frying pan on medium high heat. To test if the oil, drop a pinch of batter into the oil. If it rises immediately without changing color, then the oil is ready.

Pour ¼ cup of batter into the pan at a time, waiting for it to form a shape before pouring additional boondi. Do not make more than 4 at a time to keep the oil hot.

Fry them until the boondis are light gold in color but still soft. Remove from the oil and put them into the syrup for a few minutes before serving.

Carrot Halwa

Gajar (Carrot) Halwa, also called Gajrala, is a traditional Punjabi dessert.

Serves 4

2 cups peeled, shredded carrots
2 cups coconut milk or Mimic Crème
3 Tablespoons vegan butter or coconut oil
¼ cup vegan sugar
¼ teaspoon cardamom powder

Bring the milk/crème to a boil over medium-high heat, then reduce and simmer until it is reduced to about to 1 cup. Stir often to ensure the milk does not burn. Set aside.

Melt the butter or coconut oil in a frying pan over medium heat.

Add the shredded carrots and cook for 8 minutes or until tender and slightly changed in color.

Add the milk to the carrots and cook until it evaporates.

When almost evaporated, add the sugar and continue to cook for another three to four minutes. You will know it is ready when the Halwa starts to leave the side of frying pan.

Gulab Jamun

Gulab Jamuns are another Indian version of donuts served with syrup.

Makes 24

1 cup soymilk powder
¼ cup Gluten-Free All-Purpose flour
3 Tablespoons vegan butter
¼ cup Mimic Crème or coconut milk
½ teaspoon baking soda
2 cups of vegan sugar
1½ cups water
A pinch of cardamom powder
1 Tablespoon sliced almonds and pistachio
Oil for frying

To make syrup
In a large pan, add water, sugar, and cardamom and bring to a boil for just a minute, then remove from heat. Stir the syrup well until the sugar is dissolved, then set aside.

To make Gulab Jamun
In a bowl, mix soymilk powder, flour and baking soda. Stir to mix. Next, add the butter and mix well using a fork to cut in butter Add crème/milk. The dough should be sticky. Let the dough sit for a few minutes to allow the mixture to absorb the extra liquid. If the dough looks too dry, add a small amount of extra milk.

Grease your hands, then knead the dough. Divide into 24 equal portions and roll them into round balls.

Heat two inches of oil in a frying pan on medium heat. To test if the oil is ready, place a small piece of dough into the oil. It should only take a minute to rise. Adjust temperature if it rises too soon or too slowly.

Place no more than 6 of the Gulab Jamuns in the frying pan at a time, allowing them space to expand. Fry for 3 minutes, then turn over gently and continue to cook until they are evenly dark brown. Let the Gulab jamuns drain on paper towels for a few minutes, then add to the syrup, soaking at least 20 minutes prior to serving.

Kheer

Kheer is an Indian version of rice pudding flavored with nuts and on special occasions, saffron.

Serves

¼ cup rice
4 cups coconut milk or Mimic Crème
¼ cup vegan sugar or other sweetener
4 strands of saffron, optional
Pinch of cardamom
2 Tablespoons sliced almonds
1 Tablespoon sliced pistachios
1 teaspoon vegan butter

Place rice in a colander lined with cheesecloth or muslin. Wash rice under running water until the water appears clear.

Melt the butter in a frying pan over medium heat. Add the rice and cook for 2 minutes, just to absorb extra water.

Add the milk/crème, and cook until the rice is tender and the milk is reduced to about half. Stir often to ensure the milk does not burn or stick to the bottom of the pan.

Add the sugar, saffron if using, cardamom, almonds, and pistachios and let simmer for a few more minutes.

Turn off the heat. As it cools of will become thicker in texture.

Mohanthal

Mohanthal (sometimes spelled Mohan Thal) is wonderful Gluten-Free vegan fudge flavored with a touch of cardamom. This recipe is also best when using a candy thermometer.

Makes 16 pieces

2 cups chickpea flour
6 Tablespoons vegan butter
1 Tablespoon warm coconut milk
½ cup Mimic crème, or coconut milk with 1 teaspoon cornstarch added
1 cup soymilk powder
1 teaspoon cardamom powder
1¼ cups of vegan sugar
½ cup water
2 Tablespoons sliced almonds

Melt the butter and mix in the flour with your fingers. Keep aside for at least fifteen minutes.

Add one Tablespoon of warm milk, and use your fingers again to incorporate into the mix.

Place the crème/milk and soymilk powder in a large frying pan and cook over medium heat, stirring continuously until mixture looks like soft dough. Remove from heat and set aside.

Add the dough with the crème/milk together and cook over medium heat until it becomes light brown in color. Add cardamom.

In a saucepan, boil the sugar and water together on medium heat until syrup is 2 threads or 230°F on a candy thermometer.

Mix the syrup with flour mixture and pour on a greased cookie sheet. Do this quickly before syrup cools down. Cut the Mohanthal into 1-inch square shapes while it is still warm.

Pista Kulfi

Kulfi is a very popular Indian ice cream. It can be flavored in any way you wish, but Pistachio is the most popular version.

Serves 4

4 cups coconut milk or Mimic Crème
1 slice of Gluten-Free white bread
1 teaspoon cornstarch or arrowroot
¼ cup vegan sugar
½ teaspoon cardamom powder
10 pistachio nuts, sliced

Remove the crust from the bread and discard. Cut the bread into small pieces.

Combine the bread pieces, cornstarch, and a ½ cup of the milk in a blender, and blend until it turns into a smooth paste. Set aside.

Bring remaining milk or crème to a boil in a medium sized saucepan over medium high heat. Stir as needed to keep from burning. Let the milk boil for another 10 minutes, stirring constantly, until it reduces down to 2½ cups.

Add the bread mixture to the milk and cook for another 4 minutes, reducing the heat to medium.

Add sugar and pistachios and cook for 2 more minutes.

Turn off the heat and add cardamom powder.

Cool the milk to room temperature and pour into a bowl.

Transfer milk into a freezer-safe container. Put in freezer. It will take about 8 hours for the Kulfi to be ready to serve.

Sabudana Kheer

Sabudana Kheer is a gourmet Tapioca pudding dessert that is easy recipe to make.

Serves 4

1/3 cup tapioca
3 cups coconut milk or Mimic Crème
3 Tablespoons vegan sugar or other sweetener of choice
1 Tablespoon sliced pistachios
¼ teaspoon cardamom powder

Wash and soak the tapioca in about 1/3 cup of water for at least two hours. It will soak up most of the water and become light and fluffy.

Bring the milk/crème to a boil in heavy pan over medium heat. Boil 8 to 10 minutes, stirring frequently to prevent sticking to the bottom of the pan.

Add the tapioca, and cook until it is soft and has become translucent, about 4 minutes.

Add sugar, cardamom, and pistachios, and boil for 2 to 3 minutes. Turn off the heat. As Kheer will cool become little thicker in consistency.

Prasad

Prasad is a dessert often made for religious occasions, as prasad (offering to God). had a Sikh roommate, Sangeet, several years back and she taught me the traditional recipe of flour, honey, water, and ghee. Since ghee and honey are not vegan, I came up with this version. Do note that if you are preparing this for the religious aspects of Prasad, please consider vegan sugar or another non-animal based sweetener.

Serves 4

½ cup chickpea flour
¼ cup vegan butter
1/3 cup vegan sugar or granulated sweetener of choice
1½ cups water

Bring the water with sugar to a boil to make syrup, and Set aside.

Melt the butter in a frying pan on medium heat.

Add the flour and roast to golden brown color; stirring constantly this will take about 5 to 8 minutes.

Add the syrup slowly.

Turn down the heat to medium-low and let it simmer for another 3 minutes.

Scoop into 4 small bowls and set aside.

The flour will absorb the water as it cools.

Lassi

Lassi is an Indian yogurt drink. You can add more or less yogurt or water for a thicker or thinner beverage.

Serves 4

1¾ cups plain vegan yogurt
6 cubes ice, crushed
1½ cups ice water
2 teaspoons sweetener of choice
1 pinch salt
2 cups pureed fruit of choice, optional

In a blender, blend the yogurt, ice, water, sugar and salt until mixture becomes frothy.

Stir in optional pureed fruit. Pour mixture over ice cubes in tall glasses.

Chai Tea

This is another one of Sangeet's recipes. You can drink this hot or iced.

Serves 4

4 cups milk product of choice
1 teaspoon ground cinnamon
¾ teaspoon ground cardamom
¼ teaspoon ground ginger
¼ teaspoon ground cloves
3 black peppercorns, whole
4 black tea bags, regular or decaffeinated
Sweetener of choice, to taste

Place water, cinnamon, cardamom, ginger, peppercorns, and cloves in pot and bring to a boil. Add soymilk and return to boil.

Add tea bags. Remove from heat and cover, steeping for 5 minutes.

Strain with a cheesecloth or muslin.

Add desired sweetener.

Serve hot or chilled over ice.

Minty Lemonade

Serves 4

6 Tablespoons of freshly squeezed lemon juice
½ cup vegan sugar or sweetener of choice
¼ cup fresh mint leaves
32 oz (1 quart) cold water
Ice cubes

Chop the mint leaves.

Add lemon juice and sugar, and blend together.

Mix in water and pour the lemonade over ice

About the Author

Aruna Dawn Grey, PhD, is a Certified Holistic Health Practitioner and Doctor of Naturopathy. As part of her life journey, she sought various forms of spirituality, identifying most with the path of the Yogi. She practices the path of Raja Yoga and received initiation into Kriya Yoga with the Ananda Church of Self-Realization. A second generation disciple of Paramhansa Yoganada, she was given her name, Aruna, by Swami Kriyananda shortly after her initiation experience.

To learn more about the teachings of Paramhansa Yogananda, Kriya Yoga, and the path of Self-Realization, please visit Ananda www.ananda.org

US Recipe Measurement Conversions

Liquids, Herbs and Spices Converted

Liquids can be converted to liters or milliliters with the following table. Small volumes (less than about 1 fluid ounce or 2 tablespoons) of ingredients such as salt, herbs, spices, baking powder, etc. should also be converted with this table.

American	Metric
1 teaspoon	5 mL
1 tablespoon *or* 1/2 fluid ounce	15 mL
1 fluid ounce *or* 1/8 cup	30 mL
1/4 cup *or* 2 fluid ounces	60 mL
1/3 cup	80 mL
1/2 cup *or* 4 fluid ounces	120 mL
2/3 cup	160 mL
3/4 cup *or* 6 fluid ounces	180 mL
1 cup *or* 8 fluid ounces *or* half a pint	240 mL
1 1/2 cups *or* 12 fluid ounces	350 mL
2 cups *or* 1 pint *or* 16 fluid ounces	475 mL
3 cups *or* 1 1/2 pints	700 mL
4 cups *or* 2 pints *or* 1 quart	950 mL
4 quarts *or* 1 gallon	3.8 L

Note: In cases where higher precision is not justified, it may be convenient to round these conversions off as follows:
   1 cup = 250 mL
   1 pint = 500 mL
   1 quart = 1 L
   1 gallon = 4 L

Weights

American	Metric
1 ounce	28 g
4 ounces *or* ¼ pound	113 g
1/3 pound	150 g
8 ounces *or* ½ pound	230 g
2/3 pound	300 g
12 ounces *or* ¾ pound	340 g
1 pound *or* 16 ounces	450 g
2 pounds	900 g

Lengths

Keep in mind that 1 cm = 10 mm

American	Metric
1/8 inch	3 mm
1/4 inch	6 mm
1/2 inch	13 mm
3/4 inch	19 mm
1 inch	2.5 cm
2 inches	5 cm
3 inches	7.6 cm
4 inches	10 cm
5 inches	13 cm
6 inches	15 cm
7 inches	18 cm
8 inches	20 cm
9 inches	23 cm
10 inches	25 cm
11 inches	28 cm
12 inches *or* 1 foot	30 cm

Temperature: Fahrenheit to Celcius

Here is a quick list of the most common temperatures

300°F	148°C
325°F	162°C
350°F	176°C
375°F	190°C
400°F	204°C
425°F	218°C
450°F	232°C

Made in the USA
Lexington, KY
25 June 2012